FLIGHT PLAN

YOUR MISSION TO BECOME A MAN

Howard Graham, General Editor

THE STORY BEHIND THIS BOOK

For over twenty years, we've been developing the Flight Plan curriculum at Presbyterian Day School (PDS), an all-boys elementary school in Memphis, Tennessee. It started as an optional Bible study, but it quickly grew to a full-school curriculum centered on the seven virtues of manhood.

In 2004, Lee Burns and Chris Hill, then headmaster and chaplain of PDS, wrote the first draft of *Flight Plan*. It was expanded and updated in 2009 by Lee Burns and Braxton Brady (who first added the analogies between a boy's journey to manhood and a pilot's plan for success).

To share Flight Plan with a national audience, Braxton Brady updated and edited the book, with PDS' headmaster Steve Hancock serving as the general editor. In this latest edition, further revisions were made by Taylor Tollison and Howard Graham, the executive director of Building Boys, Making Men. We are deeply grateful for the contributions of everyone who has helped to create the book you are reading today.

In addition to major content updates, we've developed a suite of online resources for boys and their dads, teachers, and mentors; you can find those at FlightPlan.org/TakeOff. We've also published an additional book, *The 7 Virtues of Manhood*. We pray these books help many boys grow into godly young men.

Find us online for more resources and tools:
FlightPlan.org
SevenVirtues.org

Cover and Interior Design: Useful Group

ISBN: 978-1-949403-05-3

CONTENTS

A NOTE TO PARENTS   01

CHAPTER 01: PREPARE FOR TAKEOFF   03

CHAPTER 02: THE SIX MYTHS OF MANHOOD   13

CHAPTER 03: THE SEVEN VIRTUES   25

CHAPTER 04: FINDING YOUR TRUE FRIENDS   47

CHAPTER 05: RESISTING PEER PRESSURE   57

CHAPTER 06: THE DANGERS OF ALCOHOL AND DRUGS   71

CHAPTER 07: RELATIONSHIPS AND DATING   85
                (THE CHAPTER ABOUT GIRLS!)

CHAPTER 08: UNDERSTANDING PUBERTY   99

CHAPTER 09: PURITY AND PORN   113

CHAPTER 10: SCREENS, STORIES, AND SONGS   127

CHAPTER 11: LOVING YOUR FAMILY   137

CHAPTER 12: WHY SCHOOL MATTERS   151

CHAPTER 13: TARGETING TRUE SUCCESS   167

CHAPTER 14: CLEARED FOR TAKEOFF   183

A NOTE TO PARENTS

Too often, we leave boys on their own to navigate the critical transition from boyhood to manhood. We don't give them a vision of where they are going. We can put more thought into the college they get into, or the sports team they play on, than what kind of man they will become.

Without guidance, many teenage boys get lost, make poor choices, and grow up into confused and conflicted men, husbands, and fathers. The fog of the culture clouds the road to manhood. To raise our sons into men, we need to see where we are going—what men who follow God really look like.

This book offers boys a clear vision of manhood that can help them face the challenges of adolescence and make wise choices for their futures. We want to help boys see how the decisions they make today set them on a path for the men they are becoming.

We recommend that boys read this just before they enter adolescence (around age 12) and then again in the middle of their teens. This book covers the real challenges they will face, and it candidly addresses issues from relationships to drugs to puberty. Parents and mentors, please read this book alongside your boys. We hope it will serve as a starting point for an open and ongoing dialogue about growth into manhood.

Throughout this book, we have used the Bible as our foundation. We need to know the sort of men God wants boys to become. We need to understand how God wants them to respond to the challenges and opportunities they will face. However, while this book is written from a Christian perspective, we hope it is helpful to any boy embarking on the journey to manhood, regardless of his faith background.

In addition to research from some of the leading thinkers and researchers on the issues men face, this book also draws on interviews with over a thousand teenage boys and hundreds of dads. These were invaluable in giving us a first-hand glimpse into the lives, thoughts, and hearts of teenage boys. Finally, this book draws on the wisdom and experience of the Presbyterian Day School faculty, many of whom have been teaching and mentoring boys for decades.

Throughout the chapters, we have included some questions for boys to reflect on, write about, and discuss with parents or mentors. There is also a key verse at the end of every chapter; we encourage you to memorize these with your son. You can find more free discussion questions, activities, and resources at FlightPlan.org.

CHAPTER 01

Prepare for Takeoff

Roger, liftoff, and the clock is started.

Alan B. Shepard Jr., Astronaut

It was my fear that made me learn everything I could about my airplane and my emergency equipment, and kept me flying respectful of my machine and always alert in the cockpit.

Chuck Yeager, General

The engines roar so loudly that you can feel your whole body shake as the fighter jet accelerates down the aircraft carrier's short runway. You can smell the burning fuel. Standing on the deck of the carrier, you can't even see the fighter pilot inside because his plane is racing by at such an incredible speed.

Just seconds before, the jet was calmly stationed at the end of the carrier, next to a few others. But now, it's racing off the end of the runway and up into the blue sky. Where is the plane going?

Like the fighter jet, you are also heading down a short runway to take off on a great adventure with many possible destinations. During childhood, you have probably grown slowly and steadily, like a plane taxiing to the runway. But soon you will accelerate in a very intense, rapid period called adolescence. And at the end of adolescence, you will take off on an even greater adventure: manhood.

PREPARING FOR FLIGHT

Any fighter pilot will tell you that preparing well before the flight is essential to a successful mission. Every pilot spends thousands of hours learning to fly. He has considered problems he could encounter, and maneuvers he could use in those dangerous situations. He has tested and serviced the plane. He has filled it up with fuel. He has studied the flight plan, considered the weather, and learned the goal and details of the mission.

Likewise, you are a man in the making. Before you take off, it's important to make sure that you are prepared for the flight; that you know how to fly the plane and that it has fuel in it; and that you know what you will do when you come under enemy attack. And most importantly, you must know what the mission is and where you're going. It's easy to get lost in the vast sky of your future without a plan.

CHANGES ON THE WAY

So buckle up! The next few years will be a great adventure. There are several changes coming your way that you need to be prepared for:

INTELLECTUAL   You will start growing in wisdom. You will long for more independence and new challenges. You will dream new dreams and develop your own identity.

PHYSICAL   Your mind, body, and emotions will change in ways that you can't understand until you experience them. You will feel new and more intense passions and desires.

SPIRITUAL   You will begin asking more serious questions about faith and likely strengthening your relationship with God.

SOCIAL   Your relationships will look completely different. You will think about girls, your friends and your parents differently, and you will relate to them in different ways.

Did you know Jesus went through all of these same changes? Check out this verse:

> And Jesus grew in wisdom and stature, and in favor with God and man. (Luke 2:52)

Jesus grew in intellectual maturity (wisdom), physical maturity (stature), spiritual maturity (favor with God), and social maturity (favor with people). He has gone through everything you are about to go through as a boy who is becoming a man. Sometimes we forget that Jesus really was a boy. He experienced everything in the same way other boys do today.

In addition to these changes coming your way, you'll also face several challenges.

CHALLENGES ON THE WAY

Every adventure also has its share of difficulties and dangers. Self-esteem often dips during your teenage years, though many boys try to hide that by faking confidence. While you will enjoy the increasing freedoms, they will bring temptations that can be hard to resist, and a bad decision can seriously hurt you or others. While your body will grow in size and strength, it can be an awkward process with aches and acne. Girls can make your pulse race and your heart break. Adolescence can be like riding a roller coaster with many ups and downs.

In this book, we will cover the real issues and temptations that you will probably encounter. While some of these topics can be awkward or hard to talk about, it is better to know the challenges you will face ahead of time, so that you are prepared for them.

As we mentioned earlier, Jesus has been through everything you are preparing to go through. According to Hebrews 4:15, Jesus faced all of the same challenges and was tempted in all of the same ways you will be tempted, yet he did not sin. Throughout this book, we will cover a lot of ground together. Through it all, don't take your eyes off of Jesus. He is our hope, and the champion over sin and death.

Does the idea of becoming a man make you nervous, or is it something you are looking forward to? Why or why not?

_____

_____

How would you define manhood?

_____

_____

If you could have one question answered about the road ahead, what would it be?

_____

_____

QUESTIONS

YOUR PLAYBOOK

Great coaches begin the season by talking about where they want the team to be at the end of the season. They talk about conference championships and bowl games and final rankings. But they also give their players a playbook to instruct them on how they want the game to be played day by day. God has given you his playbook to help you navigate the issues that you will be facing in the next few years. Boys are often surprised to hear that the Bible speaks on so many topics. Drinking, peer pressure, friendships, families, girls, even puberty and sex—the Bible gives us perspective and instruction for all these issues.

> All Scripture is God-breathed and is useful for teaching, rebuking, correcting and training in righteousness, so that the servant of God may be thoroughly equipped for every good work.
>
> **2 TIMOTHY 3:16-17**

Most importantly, the Bible describes God's love for you. The Bible is not just a book about advice and rules—it is the true story of how much God loves us and how he saves us. It's the good news of what he has done for us, not what we do for him. You need to understand this before you read anything else in this book, so let's read that again:

The Bible is about what God has done for us, not what we do for him.

God loves you more than your dad or your mom love you, and more than your best friends love you. He loves you more than you can imagine.

Here's the hard truth: on your own, you are a mess. You were created to serve and love God, but you naturally live for yourself. God has every right to punish you for that. Instead, he chose to love you when you had nothing to offer him in return. He died for you and paid the penalty for your rebellion. And now he wants to bring you into his own family.

Here's how the Bible describes that:

> As for you, you were dead in your transgressions and sins, in which you used to live when you followed the ways of this world and of the ruler of the kingdom of the air, the spirit who is now at work in those who are disobedient. (Ephesians 2:1-2)

Even if you grew up in a Christian family, those verses describe how you were without Jesus. You were not giving God any reason to like you. You were dead. Dead people don't move, breathe, think, or do anything. They definitely don't obey; they're stuck. But then God stepped in to rescue you:

> But because of his great love for us, God, who is rich in mercy, made us alive with Christ even when we were dead in transgressions—it is by grace you have been saved.

And God raised us up with Christ and seated us with him in the heavenly realms in Christ Jesus, in order that in the coming ages he might show the incomparable riches of his grace, expressed in his kindness to us in Christ Jesus. (Ephesians 2:4-7)

God chose to love you. He saved you from your sin. He adopted you into his family. And because he loves you, he asks you to love him back.

That's not all. Now that you are part of his family, God has a mission for you. He has adventures for you, challenges for you to face, and opportunities for you to help other people. Here's what Paul says next:

For it is by grace you have been saved, through faith—and this is not from yourselves, it is the gift of God—not by works, so that no one can boast. For we are God's handiwork, created in Christ Jesus to do good works, which God prepared in advance for us to do. (Ephesians 2:9-10)

Your works—the things you do for Jesus—don't save you. But because Jesus has saved you, he has work for you to do. And he will help you do it.

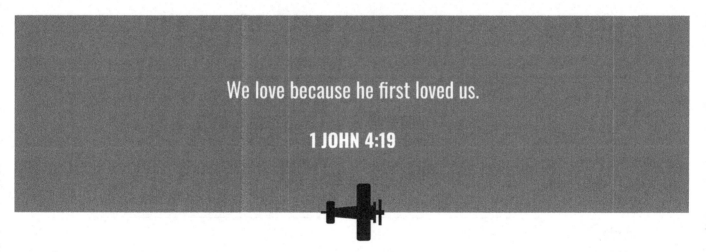

We love because he first loved us.

1 JOHN 4:19

As you think about these truths and grow in your understanding of God's love and grace, we hope that you will also grow in wisdom and stature and favor with God and people . We want you to become a godly man, husband, and father—but even before then, we hope that you will deepen your faith and walk with the Lord Jesus Christ. Even today, you can begin to explore questions about the God of the Bible.

Where do you go for advice when you are not sure what to do?

_____

_____

_____

Why did God give us the Bible? What do you think is the purpose of the Bible?

_____

_____

_____

Is your dad available to talk with you about adolescence and the journey to manhood? If he is not available, who could you talk to about this important topic?

_____

_____

_____

QUESTIONS

HOW TO GET THE MOST OUT OF THIS BOOK

Take your time and read carefully. This is your flight plan for the exciting and challenging adventure ahead. Before you begin, here are some suggestions:

- Read each chapter carefully (more than once if necessary).

- Underline, write notes in the margin, and write down any questions you might have.

- Take your time to think about and answer the discussion questions honestly.

- Discuss the book with your friends (it helps to have more than one opinion on something).

- Make sure you talk about each chapter with your father, mentor, coach, or someone you respect—with someone who has completed the mission.

- If you have the book *The 7 Virtues of Manhood*, flip back through it—those virtues will come up a lot in Flight Plan.

- Use the notes page at the end of the chapter to summarize what you have learned and memorize the key verse.

If you don't know where you want to go, then it doesn't matter which path you take.

Lewis Carroll, Author

The Christian ideal has not been tried and found wanting. It has been found difficult; and left untried.

G.K. Chesterton, Author

CHAPTER 02

The Six Myths of Manhood

In 1945, Flight 19 took off for a routine training mission. But what started as routine soon became a disaster.

Today, it is difficult for a plane to get lost. If we use GPS and other navigational technology, they will always get us back on the right path. But this technology was not available back in 1945. Pilots had to figure out their location based on where they had taken off, how long they had been flying, and how fast they were going. One little mistake in any of these calculations, and you could be lost.

Led by Lieutenant Charles Taylor, Flight 19 was the last training exercise for 13 airmen before their graduation. Six of the airmen were teenagers. The youngest airman had lied about his age to sign up for the Navy—he was just 17.

The five bombers took off from Florida and completed their exercise over the Atlantic, their last assignment before the pilots graduated. On their way back, about 90 minutes into the flight, Lieutenant Charles Taylor sent a radio transmission that his equipment was not working. He thought he was flying back to land, but his calculations were off. Instead, he was leading the five planes farther and farther out to sea.

The other pilots on the training mission tried to get Commander Taylor to change course, but he did not. Radio transmissions eventually lost the planes' signals as they kept flying in the wrong direction, and no one could ever find the planes again. Being off course cost the lives of 14 people.[1]

WHAT DOES IT MEAN TO BE A MAN?

The journey to manhood can be confusing, and the landmarks our culture provides can get us off course or even lost.

Boys today are put in a difficult situation. They are being asked to begin the journey to manhood without a clear definition of what it means to be a man. We've asked many twelve-year-olds, teenagers, and even men what it means to be a man. Not many can answer the question. Many boys today are being sent on a mission without a plan. It's no wonder that many boys end up making poor choices during their teenage years.

The world we live in offers us a selfish view of manhood. Television, videos, social media, and music teach you that you are the most important person in the world. They urge you to do what feels good, what is popular, and what makes you successful, happy, or cool.

They put athletes, musicians, and movie stars on a pedestal as our examples for what it means to be a great man. But no human is perfect, and we see more negative examples than positive. And when we base our view of masculinity on what these men do or don't do, we get a selfish and inaccurate picture of manhood.

SIX MYTHS ABOUT MANHOOD

We need a vision of the man God designed you to be. But to see that, we have to start by clearing away our wrong ideas about what it means to be a man.

We call these wrong ideas the myths of manhood. Myths are stories or ideas that aren't true, even if many people believe them. Before you can understand what real manhood looks like, you have to recognize and reject these myths of manhood. It's like becoming a good tennis player: you have to unlearn the habit of hitting a backhand the wrong way and then you can learn the proper backhand stroke.

MYTH 1—MEN DON'T SHOW EMOTION

As you grow into a man, your physical strength increases a lot. You'll probably look in the mirror as you flex your muscles. Teenage boys and men often care a lot about their strength, or at least about how strong other people think they are.

Because we care so much about our strength, we sometimes think that we are weak if we show any emotion. Just because we are tough on the outside, we feel like we have to be tough on the inside also.

Many men refuse to let anyone know they are hurting or afraid. Men often don't talk about relationships or love, believing the lie that only girls can talk about those things.

This myth can also get in the way of friendships. It's hard to develop deep friendships when you don't share the important things running through your head.

Our need for strength can even get in the way of our relationship with God. We can think we don't need anyone, including God. We might believe we can get through the day just fine by ourselves. Too many men think of loving Jesus as something weak or something women do. But that is not God's intention for you. He invites each of you into a relationship with him—a relationship where you can ask him for help, tell him what's difficult or scary, and receive forgiveness and love.

MYTH 2 - MEN ARE DEFINED BY THEIR OUTWARD ACHIEVEMENTS

Our culture judges men by outward success and achievement. We look past a person's heart and base our definition of success on grades, wealth, popularity, and athletic performance. Dr. Tim Kimmel makes some great points about the difference between success and true greatness:

- Success looks inward; true greatness looks upward, then outward.
- Success is about my agenda; true greatness is about God's agenda.
- Success is about receiving; true greatness is about giving.
- Success worships what it sees in a mirror; true greatness grieves over what it sees through its windows.
- Success pays off for now; true greatness pays off forever.[2]

Don't confuse success with true greatness. Your achievements won't give your life meaning; neither will having a big house, a prestigious job, or the "right" possessions. That stuff is how the world defines who you are. But the Bible talks about you differently. Here's what David says in Psalm 139:13-14:

> For you created my inmost being;
> you knit me together in my mother's womb.
> I praise you because I am fearfully and wonderfully made;
> your works are wonderful,
> I know that full well.
>
> **PSALM 139:13-14**

God doesn't make mistakes. He knew what he was doing when he made every part of you—even things you dislike about yourself. He knows exactly how many hairs are on your head (Matthew 10:30). He knows every thought, even if you never say it out loud (Psalm 139:2). And God loves you more than you can imagine—not because of what you do, but because of who God is.

Do not consider his appearance or his height, for I have rejected him. The Lord does not look at the things people look at. People look at the outward appearance, but the Lord looks at the heart.

1 SAMUEL 16:7

What do you think success looks like? How does the Bible define success?

_____

_____

_____

What accomplishments or activities do you use to describe yourself? Look back at the difference between success and greatness—what would it look like to be great in those areas?

_____

_____

_____

QUESTIONS

MYTH 3—MEN SHOULD ONLY PURSUE CERTAIN "COOL" HOBBIES AND INTERESTS

In some people's eyes, some passions and activities are more important or more masculine than others. Shooting a basketball is not inherently better than singing a solo. Whether you love sports or music or something else entirely, God can use your passions for your good and for his glory.

Sometimes, boys and men shy away from God-given passions and interests because of how we think other people will judge us. We may think that real boys and men don't do those things. But God is the one who gave you your talents and gifts, and he gives us the ultimate definition of manliness. Don't ignore real talents God gave you just because they don't fit some fake idea of manliness. Instead, look for ways you can use all of your talents and passions to glorify God and serve others.

As a teenage boy and man, pursue passionately the things God has put on your heart. Real men do many different things, depending on their interests and gifts. They cook and play the piano. They read and write poetry. They draw and paint. They compose music and act in plays. They play chess and go rock-climbing. They enjoy cooperative activities as much as, or more than, competitive ones. So don't listen to this myth. Discover ways you can use your gifts to love God and serve others.

MYTH 4—MEN MUST GIVE UP GREAT ADVENTURES

At your age, you have incredible adventures ahead of you. As much as you love adventures, God loves them even more. He gave boys and men with adventurous spirits. We men often enjoy exploring, taking risks, and playing games that challenge us and push us to the edge.

This sense of adventure, however, can create trouble during the teenage years. Some adventures lead down a path towards alcohol, drugs, vandalism, and sex outside of marriage. You want to avoid these destructive paths—they lead to disaster, not adventure. They can hurt you in ways that keep you from enjoying life's real adventures. So when your parents and school tell you that certain things are out of bounds, obey them. They are giving you guardrails to keep you safe.

But staying on the right path does not mean there are no adventures left to enjoy now. As you follow God, you'll have opportunities to try new things and take on new responsibilities. Maybe you can serve people in exciting ways. Maybe you can explore God's creation. Who knows where

God will take you! But no matter what he has in store for you, you can trust that the God who gave you a hunger for adventures is up to the task of planning some good ones for you.

Don't believe that lie that your adventures end at a certain age. God called men of all ages to lives of adventure. As you learn more about the character of God and his Son Jesus, you will see how God sends each of us on a great adventure when we follow him. Jesus lived a radical and adventurous life, and he calls us to live the same way.

> Somebody should tell us, right at the start of our lives, that we are dying. Then we might live life to the limit, every minute of every day. Do it! ... There are only so many tomorrows.
>
> **POPE PAUL VI**

Is there something you want to try, but you're afraid of what other people will think?

_____

_____

_____

_____

What is the coolest adventure you've ever heard of for a boy your age?

_____

_____

_____

What do you think are the "right kinds of adventure"? What makes them different from the wrong kinds?

_____

_____

_____

QUESTIONS

MYTH 5—BOYS AND GIRLS, AND MEN AND WOMEN, ARE REALLY NO DIFFERENT FROM ONE ANOTHER

God made you a boy, and he is turning you into a man. You are very different from your sister or the girl down the street. Boys and girls generally view and experience the world in different ways.

Genesis tells us that God created women and men differently. Girls' needs, the ways they prefer to communicate and to be loved, and the ways they interact with people are probably different from yours. It's not better to be a boy or a girl, but it's different. And since God made both her and you to reflect his glory, you need to understand and respect those differences.

God assigns particular roles and responsibilities to men, and he gives certain ones to women. Again, neither role is better or more important. Robert Lewis lists four responsibilities for godly men:

» Spiritual Leader

» Servant Leader

» Provider

» Protector

As men, we need to know what God expects from us, and we need to start practicing it. Too many men are passively sitting by instead of taking the initiative to lead, protect, and serve their communities and families. Know the type of leadership God expects of you and look for men who model this well so you can learn from them.

MYTH 6—YOU HAVE TO DO CERTAIN THINGS TO BECOME A MAN

In some societies around the world, it is obvious when a boy becomes a man. Usually, the boys and the men go away from their town or village on some sort of challenging adventure. They return together and have a ceremony, where everyone in the town or village recognizes that the boys are now men. Sometimes, body piercings or marks serve to remind everyone of this new status.

But in America today, there is no clear point at which a boy becomes a man. And since boys usually want to be considered men (or at least no longer children), they invent their own rites of passage into manhood. The problem is that these rituals are almost always dangerous to both your soul and your body—things like drinking, smoking, using drugs, fighting, having sex outside of marriage, joining a gang, or shoplifting.

Of course, doing dangerous things doesn't make you a man. Neither does growing older, taller, or stronger. **Every male becomes an adult, but not every adult male becomes the true man that God intends him to be.**

Growing into that man takes careful thought and planning. It takes discipline. It takes courage and endurance. It doesn't happen when your body has the capabilities of an adult man, or when you turn a certain age, or even when you get married. Becoming a real man is a lifelong adventure—and there are no shortcuts.

YOUR JOURNEY TO MANHOOD

You are about to start one of the most significant journeys of your life. You will need guides to keep you on the right path: mentors, parents, teachers, and coaches who have already trekked where you are going and can tell you where the roads lead and where the dangers lie.

There are forks in the road. You will have to make choices. There will be flashing neon signs telling you to get off the path. There will be friends who are waving you off the trail or who are hiking somewhere else. There will be apparent shortcuts, and roads that look easier than your trail. Beware of those roads, even if a steady stream of hikers are headed that way.

If you keep the map to manhood in front of you, you are more likely to become the man God wants you to be.

How do you become a man? At what point does it happen?

_____

_____

_____

Which myth of manhood are you most likely to believe?

_____

_____

_____

QUESTIONS

Summarize the most important things you've learned.

_____

_____

_____

_____

_____

_____

_____

_____

_____

Memorize and explain the key verse: Psalm 139:13-14.

_____

_____

_____

NOTES ON THE SIX MYTHS OF MANHOOD

CHAPTER 03

The Seven Virtues

Try not to become a man of success but rather try to become a man of value. He is considered successful in our day who gets more out of life than he puts in. But a man of value will give more than he receives.

Albert Einstein, Physicist & Nobel Prize Winner

Did you know airplanes have paths they follow through the sky? These are called "air routes," and they help planes follow the fastest, safest route between two airports.

But unlike roads, these routes change from day to day. For example, one flight from Berlin to New York might go north over Greenland, since the distance around the globe is shorter near the poles. But on another day, a flight from Berlin to New York might cross the Atlantic farther south, avoiding a strong headwind pushing against the plane. The route might change, but both planes are taking the best way available to get to New York.

Most commercial flights will travel from one airport to another. But private aircraft, commercial sightseeing tours, and military aircraft sometimes fly an out-and-back trip and land at the same airport from which they took off.

The journey to manhood can be the same way. Many boys follow a route carefully mapped to bring them to their destination, arriving successfully as men. But other boys take off, fly around for a while, and end up landing at the same place they took off.

This chapter will give you a clear route to follow. Following this flight plan will help you arrive at your destination: becoming a godly man. But to map your route, you need to know where your destination is. So what does it mean to be a godly man?

This chapter focuses on answering that question. In the last chapter, we looked at ways the world attempts to define manhood and exposed them as myths. Instead of these myths, here is a definition based on God's Word:

MANHOOD: A real man glorifies God by seeking an adventurous life of purpose and passion as he protects and serves others.

BEGIN WITH PURPOSE

Real manhood begins with a purpose. We were created to glorify God in all we say and do. In 1 Corinthians 10:31, Paul says, "So whether you eat or drink or whatever you do, do it all for the glory of God." No matter who you are or where you are from, your purpose is still the same—to glorify God in every situation.

Let's stop here for a second and answer two questions:

What does it mean to glorify God? It means to show the world how amazing he is. Pastor John Piper says, "'Glorifying' means feeling and thinking and acting in ways that reflect his greatness."[3] When we glorify God, we act like a mirror that reflects his greatness so that more people see it.

Why do we glorify God? God is majestic and wonderful. Think about how much he has loved you: enough to come down from heaven and die for you! Think about how incredible his creation is. He designed everything from geckos to galaxies.

Real men follow this purpose into real and meaningful adventures. A life lived for the glory of God is anything but boring. Following God will take you on journeys that might make you uncomfortable or scared. It might push you to do things that the world sees as weird or different. But one thing is sure: a life lived for the glory of God is a life of adventure.

Finally, real men live with passion. They are passionate about the things of God. Their hearts break for the things that break the heart of God. Real men use their passion and purpose to serve and protect others. Godly men seek to live a life of service to their family and community. Their passion for glorifying God leads them to stand up for those who are in need.

Godly men use God's Word as their guide. They aim to live by his standards and for his glory. The Bible tells us about the character of God. It highlights examples of behavior that delights God, and behavior that disappoints him.

Who are some examples of great men?

_____

_____

_____

_____

Choose one of them and explain why you picked him. What makes him a great man?

_____

_____

_____

_____

QUESTIONS

THE SEVEN VIRTUES OF MANHOOD

Now that we've talked about the foundation for the definition, let's look specifically at these seven virtues of manhood. Like a set of glasses to help you see the world differently, these will give you a clear vision of being a man.

Read carefully and pay close attention! This chapter will be the foundation for the rest of the book. The seven virtues are your guide in the journey to authentic manhood.

VIRTUE 1
The True Friend Stands By and Stands Up

When you think about your friends, you probably think about people you enjoy spending time with. You probably have something in common with them. You're on the same sports team, or you have math class together, or you like the same movies. Maybe you're friends because you live in the same neighborhood or because your parents are friends with their parents. You probably consider someone your friend because he is nice to you most of the time, or maybe because he makes you laugh.

A true friendship, though, is much deeper than shared interests and experiences. Godly men are willing to stick with their friends through thick and thin. True Friends endure tough times.

Like the military, real friends commit to leave no man behind. When people are hurt or struggling, it often becomes harder to be a good friend to them. If your buddy breaks his leg, you probably won't see him at soccer practice for a while. To be a True Friend to him, you might need to look for another time you can hang out. Or if something sad happens in your friend's life, he might not be as goofy or energetic as normal. To be a True Friend, you might need to change what you guys usually do together.

In today's world, most men are looking for friends who benefit them. But true friendship takes work and requires you to be selfless.

The night before Jesus was killed, he gave his disciples a new command: "Love one another. As I have loved you, so you must love one another." (John 13:34). Jesus says we should love each other as he loved us—so how did he love us? By giving up everything for us. That is a high calling!

Later that night, Jesus made this even clearer: "My command is this: Love each other as I have loved you. Greater love has no one than this: to lay down one's life for one's friends" (John 15:12-13). You probably will never have to die for your friends, but there are a lot of ways to lay down your life. When you spend time comforting a sad friend, you are laying down a few hours of your life. When you wake up early to help your friend study, you are laying down your comfort. When you stand up for your friends, you are laying down your reputation.

True Friends will give you the support you need during the challenging days of being a teenager, and they will make your life much more meaningful as a man. True friendships don't come naturally to a lot of men, but they can be one of life's greatest blessings to the man who develops them.

A HUMBLE HERO USES GIFTS FOR GOD'S GLORY

Each of you should use whatever gift you have received to serve others, as faithful stewards of God's grace in its various forms.

1 PETER 4:10

VIRTUE 2
The Humble Hero Uses Gifts for God's Glory

We live in a world with many celebrities but very few heroes. If you are like most boys, you will probably have a hard time thinking of a real-life hero other than an athlete, movie star, or musician. But being famous doesn't make someone a hero.

You can be a Humble Hero at any age. Humility doesn't mean being hard on yourself or constantly criticizing yourself—it means thinking about yourself less and thinking about God and others more. Humble Heroes know that the world is too exciting and God is too amazing to just focus on yourself all the time. Focusing on yourself is like going to a movie theater and bringing a mirror so you can look at yourself the whole time.

Instead of focusing on themselves, Humble Heroes have a heroic purpose that is bigger than themselves. Having a heroic purpose for your life means using your gifts, your time, and your energy to honor God and help others.

It's tempting to think we are responsible for all of the blessings, successes, and significance in our lives. But we can't do this on our own—we need help from God and other people. Ask God to help you be humble and put others before yourself. The Bible tells us, "God opposes the proud but shows favor to the humble" (1 Peter 5:5).

A Humble Hero doesn't live for himself. He's not chasing after a cheering crowd, a lot of money, or a comfortable life. He wants to do whatever God wants.

Just as there are many men without True Friends, there also are millions of men today without any heroic purpose for their lives. Even those who look prosperous and powerful are often bored, restless, and empty. They might have thought that the goal of life was to earn good grades, get the right job, marry a nice girl, live in a big house, and generally be a good person. All those things are good, but if that's all there is to a man's life, he will eventually realize that his life lacks a heroic purpose. The sooner you understand that you need a heroic purpose for your life, the less likely you are to end up in that place of emptiness—and the more time you will have to accomplish great things for the good of others and the glory of God.

A SERVANT LEADER TAKES INITIATIVE FOR OTHERS

Do nothing out of selfish ambition or vain conceit. Rather, in humility value others above yourselves, not looking to your own interests but each of you to the interests of the others.

PHILIPPIANS 2:3-4

VIRTUE 3
The Servant Leader Takes Initiative for Others

Many boys and men crave leadership positions. We want to be the captain of the team, sing the solo in the musical, and get elected to the student government. We aspire to lead the company, the city, and the church. Why do we want to lead? God created us in his image and told us to "subdue and rule" over the earth (Genesis 1:28). We are hardwired to create, to cultivate, to bring people together and lead them in the right direction.

But our sin twists this good leadership and makes it all about ourselves. Often, we want to lead because we believe it will make us successful. Thanks to our sin, we all tend to care more about how we can help ourselves than how we can help others. Sometimes we're drawn to leadership for selfish reasons: we get privileges and perks as leaders. Leaders are popular, and they usually make more money. They have power, and power feels good.

Servant leadership, though, centers on using the position, power, and prestige of leadership to serve other people. A Servant Leader recognizes that his relationship with Christ is first, his relationship with others is second, and he himself is third. Jesus displayed this beautifully when he served his disciples by washing their dirty feet. What an incredible example for the God of the universe, with all of his power, to get down on his knees to meet the ordinary need of someone else.

Alex and Brett Harris' book *Do Hard Things* tells the story of twelve-year-old Zach Hunter, a real Servant Leader.

When he was twelve years old, Zach Hunter was confronted with a painful fact: 27 million people around the world still live in slavery, and half of them are children. Zach's shocking encounter with that reality grew into a campaign against modern-day slavery that has taken this soft-spoken teen from the Atlanta suburbs to the main stages of the nation's largest Christian music festivals and far beyond.

Zach launched Loose Change to Loosen Chains (LC2LC), a campaign to raise money and awareness for the fight against modern-day slavery. The concept was simple: encourage his peers to gather and give their loose change, which then went to organizations working to free slaves around the world. Zach raised almost ten thousand dollars in the initial drive. Zach's plan has transformed him from a kid who suffered anxiety attacks to a sixteen-year-old who has spoken to more than half a million people at live events, appeared on national television numerous times, written two books, and even delivered a speech at the White House.

We make a difference in the lives of slaves. It doesn't really matter how young we are. It doesn't matter if we have physical, mental, or emotional disabilities. It doesn't matter the color of our skin or where we're from. Anybody can make a difference and be a voice for the voiceless.

ZACH HUNTER, AGE 16

Real men are Servant Leaders. They serve others, even when it is unpopular. Their leadership is more courageous than comfortable. It gives power to the powerless.

Servant leadership is not natural. It's the opposite of our sinful nature. It's not what the world celebrates. As a man, you will feel the pressure of competition and the need to get ahead at all costs, and it can seem like the only way to get ahead is to leave others behind. You will sometimes sense that service is not manly.

But be courageous in your leadership, and you will increasingly find yourself able to confidently make decisions that are different from what many teenagers do. You will stand firm in a sometimes uncertain world, and you will stand out as a real man.

Who is a hero to you? What makes him a hero?

_____

_____

_____

How can you be a Servant Leader at school, home, and in your community during the next month?

_____

_____

_____

QUESTIONS

Don't let anyone look down on you because you are young, but set an example for the believers in speech, in conduct, in love, in faith and in purity.

1 TIMOTHY 4:12

VIRTUE 4

The Pacesetter Sets the Example

The journey to manhood is a long race, not a short sprint. In a long race, it is vital that you run at the right speed—fast enough to meet your goals, but slow enough that you can maintain it through the whole race. You might start slower or sprint a little at the finish, but you must run most of the race at the right pace.

That's why most long races have a pacesetter, a runner who helps runners stick to a speed that's fast but that won't tire them out before the finish line. For example, some major races or elite runners will hire pacesetters to run the first part of a race at the pace of the world record, so that runners can see how close they are to setting a new record.

Being a pacesetter gives us a great picture of being an example of living for the glory of God. All the runners in the race focus on the pacesetter and adjust their pace accordingly. As we go through our days, our focus should be on Jesus Christ, the ultimate example of godly manhood. His example should set the pace for how we live day in and day out. His finished work on the cross motivates us to be an example for him in all we say and do. We can be a Pacesetter in our daily lives for those around us. We can seek to live our lives for his glory and point others to him.

On your journey to manhood, it is important for you to have a Pacesetter in your own life. While your first focus is on Christ, you will need older men in your life that you can look to as practical examples of how to live as a godly man. This might be your father, grandfather, uncle, close family friend, or mentor. It will help you to have someone who has been on the journey before you and dealt with many of the issues and situations you are facing. As you grow up, learning from a Pacesetter will also train you to become a Pacesetter for other boys who need an example.

Haven't I commanded you? Be strong and courageous. Do not be afraid; do not be discouraged, for the Lord your God will be with you wherever you go.

JOSHUA 1:9

VIRTUE 5

The Bold Adventurer Goes Courageously

Again and again in the Bible, God called a man out from where he was (often a place that is comfortable), took him on an unknown and exciting adventure, and gave him a new name. God did this with Abram who became Abraham, Jacob who became Israel, Simon who became Peter, and Saul who became Paul. God sent them to new lands. He wrestled with them. He blinded them.

Men of the Bible ventured into the wilderness and to the tops of mountains. They encountered storms and high seas, lions, and lepers. They didn't sit around all day with the ancient equivalent of the sofa and remote control. No, they dreamed and dared. They took risks. They had a wild and adventurous spirit. They allowed God to take them where he wanted and use them how he wanted. They gave their lives over to God. Being a Bold Adventurer does not mean that you drop everything and go live in the wilderness just for the sake of adventure—it means boldly facing adventures for a purpose greater than yourself.

For sixteen seasons, Baltimore Orioles shortstop Cal Ripken, Jr. never took a day off. His determination gained him the nickname "the Iron Man." His life on the field was a bold adventure. May 30, 1982 was the day Cal's streak started. Ripken started that day and every game from that point forward until the streak ended on September 20, 1998. Cal Ripken, Jr. had played an incredible 2,632 consecutive games.

When asked about the streak, Ripken once said, "As long as I can compete, I won't quit." Ripken saw his life as an adventure. He set hitting and fielding records and was one of the greatest shortstops of all time, but his greatness started with simple dedication—he committed himself to his work every day. Cal viewed his day-to-day work as an adventure, and he challenged himself to do his best every day.

Ripken's commitment to giving his best was contagious for his teammates and coaches. In fact, his work ethic and attitude influenced those outside the Orioles organization as well. Joe Torre, considered by many to be one of the greatest managers of all time said this about Ripken: "Cal is a bridge, maybe the last bridge, back to the way the game was played. Hitting home runs and all that other good stuff is not enough. It's how you handle yourself in all the good times and bad times that matters. That's what Cal showed us. Being a star is not enough. He showed us how to be more."

It seems many men have given up on adventures, settling for boredom and comfort over adventure and purpose. They assume adventures are only for teenagers or young men. They wrongly believe that they have outgrown adventures, so they work and watch TV, collect their paychecks, and grow bored and depressed. Other men, because they do not understand real adventure, pursue fake and shallow things they think will make them excited. They leave their wives and have affairs; they suddenly waste money on fancy clothes and cars; they medicate themselves with alcohol and drugs.

Growing into a man with a heroic purpose is a great adventure. Living by God's standards, rather than the world's, is a great adventure. Serving others is a great adventure.

God put an adventurous spirit in your heart. Don't sit around and let that spirit waste away.

But the noble make noble plans, and by noble deeds they stand.

ISAIAH 32:8

VIRTUE 6

The Noble Knight: Called to Duty

When you think about a knight, you probably envision a man in armor, battling another man. While knights were known for the battles they fought, they were encouraged to do so not out of a love of blood and fighting, but out of a sense of duty. They knew that, as men, they were responsible for providing for, protecting, and defending their families, friends, and communities. They were courageous in how they served others. They were willing to put their lives on the line for their beliefs.

Noble Knights lived by a code of honor and integrity. Principles, not conveniences and comforts, motivated them. They placed a high value on chivalry and civility because they understood that excellent manners showed respect to their friends, families, and communities. Families were stronger and communities were safer because of the Noble Knights who took the lead in promoting and strengthening them.

Today, many men are tempted to shrink from their responsibilities. They don't take the initiative in strengthening their families. They aren't the spiritual leaders of the family as God tells them to be. They run from conflicts; they make excuses; they leave their families. Many men honor their commitments only as long as they are convenient and comfortable. The world today doesn't always seem to give much value to honor. Cheating seems okay as long as we don't get caught and as long as the payoff is worthwhile. Many men say that manners are outdated. We often don't treat our peers and elders with much respect.

But real men are Noble Knights. They have a code of principles they are going to live by no matter what. They have integrity—they do the right thing when no one is looking. They take the initiative in providing for others and in protecting and defending their friends, families, and communities. They step up to the plate to face difficult situations. They take responsibility for their actions. They are respectful, honest, well-mannered, and courageous. You are called to duty. Go get in the action!

VIRTUE 7

The Faithful Follower: Loved By God

Have you ever seen the movie *Indiana Jones and the Last Crusade*? There is a great scene near the end of Indiana's quest to find the Holy Grail and save his father's life. To get to the Holy Grail, Indiana Jones must pass a series of tests, including the "leap of faith." You see Indiana standing on a cliff, looking across a huge chasm to an opening on the other side. He understands that is a test, but he doesn't know how he is going to cross to the other side. He thinks about it; he reads his father's notes about the test; and, with his eyes closed, he steps right off the ledge into the chasm. But as he steps off of the cliff, he lands on an invisible bridge. Once he has crossed the bridge, he throws sand on it to show everyone else the way across the gap.

Like Indiana Jones, we are faced with a big problem we can't handle on our own. There's a big gap between us and God. When God first created Adam and Eve, they lived in harmony with God. They even would take walks with God every evening. But then they rebelled against him. They rejected God and his commands. Because God is perfect, he can't go along with wrongdoing, so he sent them out of the paradise where they lived. They had shattered their relationship with God, and an enormous chasm opened up between God and people.

We can't blame Adam and Eve—we would do just the same in their place. Have you ever gone a single day without messing up or doing something wrong? So we can't fix this gap between ourselves and God.

But God made a bridge for us—the cross. When Jesus died on the cross, he solved the problem we could never solve. He offered us forgiveness and gave us a way back into relationship with God.

Almost two thousand years ago, in the days of the Roman Empire, architects constructed buildings that are still standing today. They built the Colosseum in Rome, which could hold over 70,000 people. They built bridges that stretched over hundreds of feet across steep valleys.

And they built them without the steel beams, sheets of glass, and computer calculations we use today. How? With a simple arch.

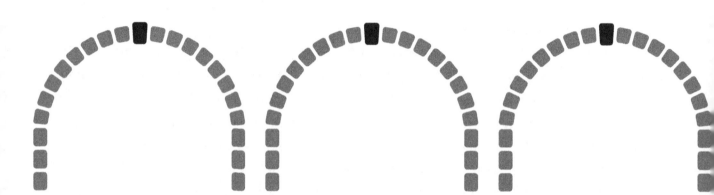

The Romans would stack angled stones on two sides so that the two stacks meet in the middle. Where those stacks met was the most important stone—the keystone. Both stacks lean on the keystone, and the weight of the keystone holds them in place. If you pulled out the keystone, the whole arch would fall apart. But with the keystone, the arch is strong enough to help support an enormous bridge or wall.

Being a Faithful Follower is the keystone for true manhood. If we aren't getting our strength and joy from Jesus, all of our effort to be good will crumble. We aren't strong enough to hold ourselves up on our own. But when we have Jesus' love and forgiveness at the center of our lives, we can be true men who love others, have noble adventures, and serve their communities.

Following Christ and living for the glory of God takes faith in something we cannot see. In 2 Corinthians 4:18, Paul tells us, "So we fix our eyes not on what is seen, but on what is unseen, since what is seen is temporary, but what is unseen is eternal." Just as Indiana Jones couldn't see the bridge, we can't see God's forgiveness. It's not something we can touch or look at. We have to have faith that Jesus died to pay for our sins. And we have to have faith that he deserves all of our love and all of our life. If you aren't sure if you have faith, talk to God about it. Ask him to help you believe that what he says is true.

When you accept Jesus Christ as your personal Lord and Savior, God counts you as perfect because of what Jesus did on the cross. But that's not all! He makes you part of his own family, and he helps you to follow him.

True believers are Faithful Followers. They faithfully follow Jesus' leading regardless of the circumstances. Sometimes this can involve facing danger. Jesus taught his disciples, "If anyone wants to follow after me, let him deny himself, take up his cross, and follow me. For whoever wants to save his life will lose it, but whoever loses his life because of me will find it" (Matthew 16:24-25). Being a Faithful Follower can be tough, but God is with us as we take steps of faith every day. If we trust that God keeps his promises, then we can live out our faith with confidence.

The more you understand and experience God's love and forgiveness, the more joy you will find in your life—knowing that all your sins, including the ones you will commit as a teenager and as a man, have been forgiven. This joy will fuel your desire to live your life in a way that is pleasing to God, following him faithfully every day of your life.

At your school or in your community, what problems do you see? What seems wrong or unfair to you? What can you do about it?

_____

_____

_____

QUESTIONS

Which virtues do you think come naturally to you? Is there a virtue that is especially challenging for you?

_____

_____

_____

THE VISION HAS BEEN SET BEFORE YOU:
1. A True Friend Stands By and Stands Up
2. A Humble Hero Uses Gifts for God's Glory
3. A Servant Leader Takes Initiative
4. A Pacesetter Sets the Example
5. A Bold Adventurer Goes Courageously
6. A Noble Knight Lives Honorably
7. A Faithful Follower is Loved by God

Godly men develop true friendships by leaving no man behind. They understand their purpose and establish a God-sized vision for their life. They serve others by giving up control of their lives to God and realizing they come third. Real men use their passions to glorify God and make a difference in their community. Godly men are called to duty. They seek to serve and protect others. Real men don't sit around, but instead lead adventurous lives. They allow God to use them where he wants and how he wants.

THE ONLY PERFECT MAN

The Bible tells us about the only man ever to lead a perfect life: Jesus Christ. As a man, Jesus faced many of the struggles and temptations that you will encounter. He surrounded himself with friends, and he cared deeply about those friends. They presented him with some bad ideas; they disappointed and betrayed him. But Jesus kept loving them anyway.

Jesus was tempted to use his power and popularity for his own comforts and convenience rather than serving others. He felt many of the emotions that you do: sadness and frustration, joy and laughter, disappointment and fulfillment. He knows firsthand the struggles and temptations you will face, but he also knows the sort of man you can become.

Jesus didn't come only to set an example for you. He lived and died for you. He took the punishment for your sin and gave you the credit for his perfect life. If you have trusted in Jesus, he has taken away all of the grime and dirt of your sin and clothed you in his perfect righteousness. Here's how Paul describes you in Ephesians 2:1-5

> As for you, you were dead in your transgressions and sins, in which you used to live when you followed the ways of this world and of the ruler of the kingdom of the air, the spirit who is now at work in those who are disobedient. All of us also lived among them at one time, gratifying the cravings of our flesh and following its desires and thoughts. Like the rest, we were by nature deserving of wrath. But because of his great love for us, God, who is rich in mercy, made us alive with Christ even when we were dead in transgressions—it is by grace you have been saved.

That is amazing news! If you trust in Jesus as your Savior, he forgives every wrong thing you have done. He sets you free from the control of selfishness and sin. He brings you into his own family.

But it doesn't stop there—he also invites you and helps you to love and serve him. You are not just some kid God rescued; you are a soldier in his army. You get to join him on his mission of showing his love to the whole world. Here's what Paul says next:

> For it is by grace you have been saved, through faith—and this is not from yourselves, it is the gift of God—not by works, so that no one can boast. For we are God's handiwork, created in Christ Jesus to do good works, which God prepared in advance for us to do. (Ephesians 2:8-10)

43

Pay attention, because Paul's making an essential point here. You aren't saved by what you do. You are saved by what God has done. But now that God has saved you, he has an exciting mission for you! God created you, so he knows exactly what you are good at and what you love, and he has planned out good works specifically for you.

We hope this vision of what it means to be a man will guide your journey to manhood. We hope it assures you, encourages you, and gives you hope. Now that you know what it means to be a man, let's see how you can live that out as you encounter the exciting yet dangerous challenges, opportunities, and temptations of the years to come, starting with friends and peer pressure.

Summarize the most important things you've learned.

_____

_____

_____

_____

_____

_____

_____

Memorize and explain the key verse: 1 Corinthians 10:31.

_____

_____

_____

NOTES ON THE SEVEN VIRTUES

CHAPTER 04

Finding Your True Friends

My best friend is the one who brings out the best in me.

Henry Ford, Founder of Ford Motor Company

It was 1952, and fighter pilot Robinson Risner was flying his F-86 over North Korea with his wingman, Lt. Joe Logan, alongside him.

Already a jet ace—an elite title meaning he had shot down five enemy aircraft— Risner was escorting bombers in an attack on a chemical plant when the fuel tank of Logan's plane was hit.

Without fuel, Logan's plane was powerless. Instead of letting Logan crash in enemy territory, Risner attempted a dangerous move. He nosed his plane into the back of Logan's and pushed him 60 miles through heavy enemy flak to an Air Force detachment where he could bail out safely. It was a heroic feat.[4]

In your life, you will need friends who are willing to push you along when you cannot make it yourself. True Friends "leave no man behind" even if it means taking a risk. The upcoming years will be difficult, and you will need solid friendships to help you get through them.

"Who are my friends? Why are they my friends? Will my closest friends be in my class?" It's natural to spend a lot of time thinking about friendships—most days, you spend more time with them than with your family. For the first time, you are starting to build a life outside of your parents. And it is your friends who are shaping that life.

WHY MEN (AND BOYS) NEED FRIENDS

You need friends at every stage of life, but it is probably during these teenage years that you will first realize how crucial they are. Think about the benefits of having friends:

- » They provide companionship and keep you from being lonely
- » They make you laugh
- » They give you the confidence to try new things and grow
- » They validate and encourage you
- » They teach you relationship skills
- » They offer support
- » They provide stability in a changing world and at a time of great changes in your life

There are many advantages to having friends, but it's okay if you don't yet have a True Friend as we will define it in this chapter. It takes a lot of maturity and time to develop deep and meaningful friendships.

> A friend loves at all times,
> and a brother is born for a time of adversity.
>
> **PROVERBS 17:17**

Even if you don't have a True Friend yet, keep working to develop the right type of friendships and then be patient. Know that a True Friend can come from various places, including from your own family. And there's not a right number of friends to have. As with so many other things, the quality of friendships is more important than the quantity.

WHAT TRUE FRIENDSHIP LOOKS LIKE: JONATHAN AND DAVID

Most guys your age do not understand what it means to be a True Friend. We tend to base our friendships on what the world values rather than what God values.

But the Bible gives us a great example of true friendship. Jonathan and David were two young men close to your age who developed a true friendship based on things much more significant than similar interests and backgrounds.

After the teenaged David, killed the Philistine giant Goliath, he developed a true friendship with Jonathan, the son of King Saul, whose people had been threatened for years by the Philistines.

The first thing to note about their relationship is their very different backgrounds. Jonathan was the son of the king: a prince. He had privilege, prestige, power, and money. He grew up in a palace.

David was a shepherd from a very ordinary family—in fact, he was probably poor. David and Jonathan seem to have had nothing in common. If they were alive today, they wouldn't go to the same school, live in the same neighborhood, or play on the same teams. Their friendship—one of the best examples of true friendship in the Bible—teaches us that having the same background or interests isn't the basis for a true friendship.

Don't judge someone's potential for being a True Friend on whether or not he is similar to you. It's good to have friends of different backgrounds, races, interests, and resources.

Since Jonathan and David didn't have similar backgrounds, they built their friendship on something else: on trust, shared beliefs, and serving each other. These are characteristics of true friendship.

FIVE TRAITS OF TRUE FRIENDS

So what does it mean to be a True Friend? The examples of friendships God gives us are different than most friendships you will have as a teenager. They are not based just on doing things together or on having the same interests.

Here are some characteristics that True Friends need:

True Friends sacrifice. David and Jonathan sacrificed for one another. When God decided that David would be the next king, that meant Jonathan would not inherit the throne after all. But instead of fighting David for the throne, Jonathan gave David his own bow, sword, and armor. True Friends value the friendship more than their own success or popularity. Would you happily see your friend chosen over you for a part in the school play or a position student government? Would you give a friend something that costs you a lot?

True Friends tell each other about whatever is on their hearts. They share fears and hopes. They talk about God. Friends speak the truth gently but honestly, and they comfort each other. They don't just send text messages—they make time to talk face to face. They talk about meaningful things. If there's something stressful or sad in your life, do you have a friend that you can share that with? Can you tell your friend that he is doing something wrong, when he is hurting himself or others? Are you willing to listen to your friend if they are having trouble?

True Friends display unfailing kindness. Jonathan asks David, "Show me unfailing kindness like the LORD's kindness as long as I live" (1 Samuel 20:14 NIV). That's not kindness only when it's convenient. That's not partial kindness. When was the last time you did something genuinely kind for a friend? When did you last do something for a friend that meant giving up something you wanted?

True Friends serve each other. At the Last Supper, Jesus washed the feet of his closest friends, the disciples. He then asked his disciples in John 13:12, "Do you understand what I have done for you? You call me teacher and Lord, and rightly so, for that is what I am. Now that I, your Lord and teacher, have washed your feet, you should also wash one another's feet. I have set you an example that you should do as I have done for you." Are you willing to serve your friends even if it means being uncomfortable or sacrificing your reputation?

True Friends are loyal. They stick with each other no matter the circumstance. Both David and Jonathan loved the Lord and sought to follow his commandments. Their loyalty to God bound them to one another. Are you willing to give up something so you can be there for your friend? When someone talks badly about your friends, do you stick up for them, or do you just let it go?

Eventually, you will have to make a choice: loyalty to a friend or loyalty to your popularity. If you don't have the courage to stand up for a friend when he is being picked on, you are not a True Friend. And if you can't stand up for your friend, don't expect him or others to stand up for you. Friends protect each other like Noble Knights. They are loyal and courageous.

Why do you have the friends that you do? What do you look for in a friend?

_____

_____

_____

Do you talk with your friends about important or emotional issues, or do you keep those hidden?

_____

_____

_____

QUESTIONS

WHO ARE YOUR TRUE FRIENDS?

As a teenager, you may experience friendships that disappoint and hurt you, friendships that come and go, and friendships that can lead you astray. So how do you know who your real friends are? It can be helpful to think about different types of friends and different groups of friends. Here's one way of thinking about the types of friends you have:

1. **Not Your Friend:** People you usually don't hang out with.
2. **Acquaintances:** People you might see in one activity or place—maybe at school or church or on a sports team—but you don't usually talk to outside of that.
3. **Wannabe Friends:** People you might want to be friends with for the wrong reasons, like their popularity or money (wannabe friends are not your True Friends, because your friendship is only based on what you want out of it).
4. **True Friends:** People that you trust and confide in because you know that they have your best interests in mind. (If you choose your friends wisely, these friends are the ones whose influence on your life makes you a better person.)

Who are your True Friends? They will make a big difference in the man you become. Your friends will shape what you think and do and say. The Bible tells us that bad company corrupts good character, so pick your friends wisely (1 Corinthians 15:33). Don't be afraid to lovingly hold them accountable and to respectfully point them in the right direction. But if your friends are leading you away from becoming a godly man, don't be afraid to let go of those friendships. You don't want to settle for just any friendship—you need the right kind of friendship.

WHEN FRIENDS AREN'T ENOUGH

Even True Friends will let you down sometimes. Don't shy away from telling a friend how he hurt you or disappointed you. Talk to your friends honestly and forgive your friends when they apologize. Ignoring disappointments in your friendships and holding onto grudges can end many meaningful friendships. When you hurt a friend, apologize and ask for his forgiveness as well.

You will also need some time alone as a teenager. Don't be afraid of being alone. It doesn't mean you're weak or unpopular. Jesus often retreated from his friends and the crowd to be by himself and to pray. You don't have to fill up every minute with friends or activities.

Sometimes, we stay so busy with friends and scheduled activities that we neglect our souls and our relationship with God. Spend quiet time each day reading the Bible and praying. Spend time each day reading, thinking, and relaxing. Your life will have better balance, and your friendships will be stronger. Good friendships depend more on what kind of time you spend together than on how much time.

It is never too early to start seeking out true friendships. The upcoming years will be full of challenges, but they will be much easier if you have some "wingmen" who are willing to fly with you through the good and the bad. Even more significantly, you will experience a lifetime of the rich joys that True Friends can bring. God built us for connection with each other, and being a man means entering into true friendships.

Think about the guys you spend the most time with. Are they True Friends or shallow friends?

_____

_____

_____

Are you a True Friend to others? Look back at the five traits of a True Friend. Which one of those do you want to work on this week?

_____

_____

_____

QUESTIONS

Summarize the most important things you've learned.

_____

_____

_____

_____

_____

_____

_____

_____

_____

Memorize and explain the key verse: Proverbs 17:17.

_____

_____

_____

NOTES ON THE SIX MYTHS OF MANHOOD

CHAPTER 05

Resisting Peer Pressure

I firmly believe that respect is a lot more important, and a lot greater, than popularity.

Dr. J, Julius Irving, Hall of Fame Basketball Player

It takes a lot of work to become an astronaut. No one knows that better than Captain Jeremy Hansen.

Captain Hansen was a pilot for the Canadian Air Force, but he set his sights on becoming an astronaut. He knew it would be a difficult challenge—there were 5,300 other people who had the same dream and who were trying out for the same spot. But that didn't stop him from trying.

Captain Hansen and the 5,300 other applicants had to pass a series of tests that would push them to their limits. They had to put out fires in extreme heat. They had to save a sinking ship in icy water. The Canadian Air Force tested the limits of their endurance and their ability to work with others.

Captain Hansen made it through all of the tests and ended up at the top of the class. And on May 13, 2009, he was officially selected to become an astronaut in the Canadian Space Agency.

When he was asked about how he survived the brutal tests, he pointed back to his pilot training: "I don't think I'd be in this position without my Air Force experiences. My military flying and my fighter flying has taught me how to react to being under pressure. On a regular basis, I'm asked to perform while I'm flying a fighter jet under dynamic and stressful situations."[5]

In the upcoming years, you will face many challenges. Without a plan, you will inevitably find yourself flying off course and into potential danger. Like Captain Hansen, you will need to rely on your training to get through. In this chapter, you'll learn the information and strategies you'll need to navigate peer pressure.

What is peer pressure? It is social pressure from your peers—your classmates and friends your age— to take certain actions, adopt certain values, or otherwise conform to be accepted. Peer pressure is powerful. Everyone feels it, even adults—but it is most powerful during the next few years of your life.

Over the next few years, you will feel a pressure, to be just like everybody else and to do what they are doing. You will be pushed to please your buddies and classmates more than your parents or other adults. You will want your looks, clothes, and possessions to be like those of your classmates (which will probably be based on what you see in the movies, TV, and online, and on your observation of teenagers a little older than you).

Even if you don't realize it, people change you when you spend time with them. You learn from them, and they learn from you. That is why it's so important to build true friendships with other boys who are on the road to becoming real men.

During your teen years, you will also have more freedom to follow peer pressure. You will be tempted to do a lot of things—not just to show your independence, but to make your peers like you more. Dealing with these pressures can be hard sometimes.

SIX PRESSURE POINTS

What does it look like to face peer pressure? Here are six areas you might be pressured in:

Stress: We are all pressured to be in a hurry. You have homework to finish, a musical instrument to practice, a sports team to play on, and friends who want to hang out with you. You'll feel pressure to deal with crammed schedules, and to establish and maintain relationships. You might have to navigate a sometimes tricky or painful home life. You may feel like you have too much going and can't do it all, which creates a lot of stress.

The In Crowd: One of the most important decisions you will make in life is who you surround yourself with. You will feel pressured to be a part of groups that might not have the same beliefs or values you do. These groups may tempt you to use foul language, watch inappropriate movies, cheat, vandalize or steal, and disrespect your parents or lie to them. Just because someone is popular doesn't mean he is a good fit for you.

Body Image: Body image is your idea of what your body looks like. How you see yourself shapes much of how you feel about yourself. Flip through a magazine or sit through a movie, and you face a tidal wave of unrealistic images of the "perfect" guy or girl. Sometimes girls wrongly believe that being super skinny will make them more appealing. For guys, it may be about looking stronger. But look around—there are all kinds of people in the world. And nearly all of us have something about themselves they don't like.

Opposite Sex: There can be intense pressure for guys when it comes to sex. Sometimes the temptation is to talk inappropriately about girls, especially about their bodies. Maybe the temptation is to make up things about a girl that aren't true. A lot of guys are tempted to look at pornography. Sometimes it might seem like everyone in high school (and on TV) is talking about who has sex and who doesn't. Unfortunately, some teens feel that they have to have sex in order to keep dating someone or to be accepted. And that's not true. We'll talk more about that in future chapters.

Drugs and Alcohol: You will encounter occasions to use alcohol, tobacco, and drugs. Plan in advance for how you will respond, and ask your parents or other trusted adults if you have questions.

Movies, music, the internet, and your school hallways don't always accurately portray the risks of drug or alcohol use. We'll talk more about this soon as well.

Bullying: There are many ways that young people tease or bully each other, even if they don't realize it at the time. Bullying can be direct attacks like punching, teasing, name-calling, intentionally hurting a classmate, tearing down someone's reputation or taunting someone online. But it can also include spreading rumors or encouraging others to exclude someone. If someone pushes you to pick on somebody else, stand your ground. Speak up and defend the person being picked on (whether people are talking about them to their face or behind their back).

What are these situations likely to look like? Let's walk through a few examples.

Scenario #1: It's Friday night; you and one of your friends are spending the night with another buddy. At some point, you start talking about other classmates. Your best friend starts making fun of Bill: "He's a loser," or "No girl is ever going to like him," or "Do you know what so-and-so said about him?" Your friends are laughing at how pathetic they think this guy is. What do you do? Why?

_____

_____

_____

Scenario #2: One of your friends at school is having a party. It's a great party with lots of girls, good music, and your closest friends all there. At 10:00, your buddy Tucker shows you and two girls what he's got in his backpack: a bottle of whiskey. He pours some whiskey into his Coke. "Now this is the joy of cola," he says, and he pours some for Lauren and Sophie. Lauren is a girl that you and about a dozen other guys really like. Jackson reaches for your cup as he prepares to pour some whiskey into your drink. What do you do? Why?

_____

_____

_____

Scenario #3: You just took the big history test, and you're having lunch with two of your good friends. They take the test later that afternoon. Jack tells you he didn't have a chance to study very much for the test. Paul needs to make a good grade, or he may be suspended from the basketball team for low grades, and his parents might ground him. "What's on the test?" one of them asks. "Help us out." What do you do? Why?

_____

_____

_____

Which of these scenarios would be hardest for you? Why?

_____

_____

QUESTIONS

If you could read people's thoughts about you, would you want to? Why or why not?

_____

_____

QUESTIONS

What types of peer pressure have you already faced?

_____

_____

THE CAUSE OF PEER PRESSURE

Understanding the real cause of peer pressure can help you to avoid some traps and relieve some of your anxieties. Psychologists tell us that at the most basic level, conformity and peer pressure mostly relate to the insecurities and inferiorities we feel.

Satan wants us to think poorly of ourselves and to forget the incredible value and worth we have in God's eyes. We believe we are not attractive, talented, or smart. That means that we don't feel good about ourselves, even if on the outside we appear happy, confident, successful, and handsome. If you could hear the thoughts of many teenagers, you'd probably be surprised at how little they like themselves.

So many things are in the process of changing for a teenager—body, mind, friends, identity, values, and more. This can make them you uncomfortable and unsure of yourself. It's often an awkward time when you get cut from teams and realize, maybe for the first time, that there are people more talented than you are. You may think you are too skinny or too fat, that your voice is too deep or too squeaky, that you're uncomfortable with girls, and that everyone is staring at that zit on your face. Many teenagers hide these things by trying to be just like everyone else.

And as you begin to feel the urge to break away from your childhood relationship with your parents, it is also natural that you seek closer relationships with your friends. They become a bigger factor in your decision making. They will be with you when you face a big decision related to peer pressure.

> We often ask ourselves, "How could the early disciples turn the world upside down when millions of Christians can't even keep it right side up today?" The answer is simple. They didn't conform their faith to the world. They had the truth, and they refused to water it down. They held a faith that would not compromise.
>
> **BILLY GRAHAM,** EVANGELIST

EFFECTS OF NEGATIVE PEER PRESSURE

Peer pressure can be positive or negative. Unfortunately, during the teenage years, it is harmful more often than it's helpful. What does negative peer pressure do?

» It can cause you to make poor decisions that harm yourself and others.
» It can cause you to make decisions that change your life forever.
» It can cause you to make a deadly decision.
» It limits your ability to be a leader.
» It can lead you away from God and add roadblocks on your journey to becoming the man God wants you to be.

If you are a follower of Christ, you are called to lead a different life than the one the world tells you to live. Your behavior and customs should stand out—they should follow God's instructions for your life. God's Word and the Holy Spirit renew your mind; they change the way you see the world and how you live in the world. Colossians 3:2 says, "set your minds on things above, not on

> Do not conform to the pattern of this world, but be transformed by the renewing of your mind. Then you will be able to test and approve what God's will is—his good, pleasing and perfect will.
>
> **ROMANS 12:2**

earthly things." Studying the Scriptures renews our minds and helps us view the world differently.

What about you? Do you think about the world differently than your peers? Do you have different values than what you see on TV shows?

We will be tempted to follow the behaviors, values, and patterns of the world. Jesus was tempted by Satan in the desert. He was offered the things that so often tempt us: power, popularity, and possessions. He stayed firm and focused on worshipping and serving the Lord.

PROTECTING YOURSELF FROM PEER PRESSURE

Why does it matter if we want to be like our friends? It depends on what your friends are doing. It's probably not a big deal to wear the same jeans as all your friends, but polluting your body with cigarettes to be like them is a much different matter.

So what are some practical things you can do to limit your vulnerability to peer pressure and make the sort of decisions that are pleasing to God? Here are some principles and tips.

Get your worth from God. If you remember that God created you, loves you, and is willing to forgive you through Jesus Christ, then you know that you're incredibly valuable to God, so you don't need to find your value from other people. Lots of people try to use worldly things to fill up a hole they have inside. Only God can fill that emptiness. Until you understand that, you will be trying to fill that hole with other people's approval, which will make you vulnerable to peer pressure. As much as you like your friends, you don't depend on them for your value. You don't need to do dangerous or unwise things to earn your friends' respect—you already have God's everlasting love that he demonstrated on the cross of Christ (Romans 5:8).

Get advice and encouragement from your parents. Tell them about the peer pressure you are facing. They were teenagers once, too, and their wisdom and support can be helpful. Rehearse with them what you'll say in difficult situations. Also, use them to bail you out of parties where there is drinking or drugs. Work out a plan (or even a code word) to let them know you need to be picked up.

Have a friend who holds you accountable. In your battle with peer pressure, friends make a huge difference. Find at least one friend with whom you will share a commitment about the sort of choices you will make as a teenager. Ask him to make these same commitments to you, and then hold each other accountable. If one of you starts to stray from the right path, it is the responsibility of the other friend to point this out in a loving but firm way. Be there for each other and stand up for each other. Having a buddy gives you courage in hard situations.

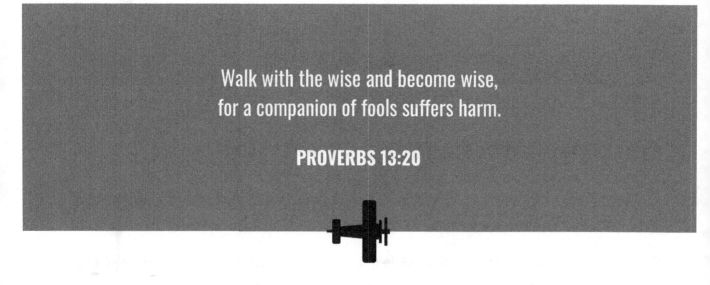

Walk with the wise and become wise,
for a companion of fools suffers harm.

PROVERBS 13:20

Choose your friends carefully. While it is important to encourage straying friends to make wise choices, there are some times when it is wise to break off certain friendships, either temporarily or permanently. If your friends are dragging you down the wrong path, then they are not True Friends, and you should find new ones. It is normal and natural that your friend group changes as you move from elementary school through middle school and into high school.

Ask an older person to mentor you. Real men know they don't have all the answers. They meet with older men who serve as mentors to them—wise, godly men who have life experiences that the younger men do not yet have. A mentor can talk with you about your grades, peer pressure, girlfriend, sports, spiritual growth, work ethic, friends, and relationships with your family. You can ask them questions and hear their advice. Don't wait until you are already grown up—ask an adult to be a mentor to help you in your journey to manhood. And as you grow up, look for opportunities to serve as a mentor to guys who are younger than you.

Decide in advance what you will say and do in situations involving negative peer pressure. In the next chapter, we'll talk specifically about drugs, alcohol, and other situations that can pressure you to make a dangerous choice. If you have not already decided in advance what you will say and do, it will be easy to make the wrong decision in the heat of the moment. Know what you will say. Practice saying no. Practice it with a parent, friend, or mentor. That way, it won't be as hard when the real test comes. If your friends realize that you are committed to saying no, they may be less likely to tempt you later.

> Do not love the world or anything in the world. If anyone loves the world, love for the Father is not in them. For everything in the world—the lust of the flesh, the lust of the eyes, and the pride of life—comes not from the Father but from the world.
>
> **1 JOHN 2:15-16**

Be yourself. Let go of the need to be cool. God created you exactly the way you are. Accept your differences; rejoice in them. Don't pretend to be someone you are not. It dishonors God, and it takes a lot of your energy to be an actor. Being fake is tiring and will eventually drive people away anyway. If someone can't accept you for who you are, then you should look for other friends.

Don't tease others or stand by silently when it happens. Over the next few years, you will probably see more guys making fun of people. Much of it is an attempt to fit in and feel cool. Most of it will be more verbal than physical. Don't underestimate the pain that you and your classmates can cause, even if the person they are teasing seems like he is handling it okay. If you see bullying, don't stand by and let it happen; stop it. Real men—Noble Knights—defend the weak. It can take just one person standing up for a ridiculed classmate to change the whole dynamic. Be that person: be a leader.

As with all of the teenage issues you will face, if you have the finished product in mind—the sort of man God designed you to be—your responses to peer pressure will fall into place.

Think about the virtues of manhood at the start of this book. If you understand what it means to be a True Friend, you won't settle for the superficial things that most people think equal friendship. If you have a heroic purpose for your life, you'll see how silly so many of the teenage issues are, and you'll see how quickly they can sidetrack the real goal of your life. If you seek out bold adventures for your life, you'll see that many of the typical teenage "adventures" are shallow by comparison. If you are a Servant Leader, you'll understand that going against the crowd is leadership and that by setting a godly example, you are serving your friends. And if you are a Noble Knight, you will protect and defend your community of friends. You will be motivated to exert positive peer pressure based on the sort of moral community God wants for us.

If you can resist negative peer pressure now, you will be a man who is more likely to resist pressure. Peer pressure doesn't end when you turn 20. Many men spend their time and energy trying to create an image to impress others. It's almost always an image conformed to the things of this world, and although it looks good on the outside, it usually leads to hollowness on the inside.

Resisting peer pressure is not easy. You will need God's help. Ask him to give you the wisdom and courage to make the sort of choices he wants for you.

Living for the glory of God is tough, and you will inevitably mess up. In fact, many of you reading this have already experienced some turbulence on your flight. Your flight might have taken a different route because of a bad decision you made or a situation that you couldn't control. Regardless of how many times you have messed up in your journey, it is never too late to chart a new course. The good news is that God's grace is bigger than any of our mistakes. He promises to give us a new heart. We just have to ask him.

Are you doing anything now to renew your mind—to see the world the way God sees it?
What can you do this week to renew your mind?

_____

_____

_____

What does it mean to be yourself?

_____

_____

_____

QUESTIONS

NOTES ON RESISTING PEER PRESSURE

Summarize the most important things you've learned.

_____

_____

_____

_____

_____

_____

_____

_____

_____

Memorize and explain the key verse: Proverbs 13:20.

_____

_____

_____

CHAPTER 06

The Dangers of Alcohol and Drugs

In drunkenness, we retreat and surrender to sin inside of us, accepting that broken me is the real me I'll always be. In the Spirit, we cleanse and advance ourselves with real truth, grace, hope, and joy, not artificial and expiring counterfeits.

Marshall Segal, Author

In November 2009, Yves Rossy, a 50-year-old Swiss adventurer and former fighter pilot, attempted to soar from Morocco to Spain on jet-powered wings. Rossy took off from Tangiers in Morocco, but about four minutes into the flight, he hit turbulence. He flew into such a thick bank of clouds that he couldn't tell which way was up.

When he broke out of the clouds, he found himself dropping at up to 180 miles per hour until he was just 2,500 feet above the water. Hitting water that fast would have felt like hitting concrete, and he was 20 seconds away from impact. "So the sea comes very fast," he said. "Unstable, at this height, there is no playing anymore. So I throw away my wing and opened my parachute." Thanks to his parachute, Rossy ditched safely into the Atlantic.[6]

In the next few years, you'll face temptations that look like exciting adventures—but those adventures can quickly become dangerous. To avoid that, you can start preparing now for two big temptations.

The first is to drink, smoke, and use other drugs. (We'll talk about the second temptation, sex, in a few chapters.) It's natural to be curious about those things and have lots of questions:

- » Why do so many people drink?
- » What does beer taste like? What does it feel like to smoke?
- » My parents or adults I know drink, so how can there be anything wrong with drinking?
- » What's it like to be high? Will life be more fun if I'm drunk or stoned or on drugs?
- » Won't I be more of a man if I drink and smoke? Will I feel things more intensely if I try drugs?
- » Won't I fit in better with my friends or be more relaxed with girls if I drink and smoke pot?

If you haven't wrestled with these questions yet, you probably will soon. And you'll likely have opportunities to drink, smoke, and use drugs. A classmate may sneak a bottle of vodka to a party and pour shots into soft drinks. A classmate might invite you to the parking lot at the school dance to smoke a joint. You'll spend the night at a friend's house, and he might suggest that you get some beers from the refrigerator in the garage. You and your buddies will meet a few girls at the movie theater, and they could pull out some cigarettes from their purses and suggest that you all go behind the theater to smoke. Some of your classmates, probably even some of your friends, will drink, smoke, and use other drugs in the upcoming months and years.

What about you? What will you do? We'll talk about each of these temptations in this chapter, but let's start with alcohol.

HOW ALCOHOL WORKS

Before we talk about your choices about alcohol, you need to know how alcohol works, both so that you understand its dangers now and so you can be responsible if you choose to drink when you are 21.

There are three basic categories of alcohol: beer, wine, and hard liquor. A cocktail is a drink mixing hard liquor(s) with other ingredients like syrups, soda, or fruit.

Different alcoholic drinks have different amounts of alcohol (ethanol) in them, even if they are the same size. 12 ounces of most beers, 5 ounces of wine, and 1.5 ounces of hard liquors all have about the same amount of alcohol. That means that a tiny amount of hard liquor can affect someone even more than a 12-ounce beer.

Alcohol's effect will also differ from person to person. The less you weigh, the longer it's been since you've eaten, and the less frequently you drink, the more strongly alcohol will affect you.

WHAT THE BIBLE SAYS ABOUT DRINKING ALCOHOL

Christians can interpret passages from the Bible differently and make different decisions about alcohol. As long as Christians are basing their decisions on the Bible, they can come to different views that all deserve our respect. However, getting drunk is a sin and brings on all sorts of problems. Getting drunk is a misuse or abuse of a gift from God and causes you to make poor decisions. Let's see what the Bible says about drinking too much: "Do not get drunk on wine, which leads to debauchery. Instead, be filled with the Spirit" (Ephesians 5:18).

So adults who can legally enjoy God's gift of a drink should only do so in moderation. God cautions us that drinking too much leads to big problems. Adults should not drink if it will be a stumbling block to other people or encourage someone else to head down a dangerous path.

Adults should also consider whether or not it is wise for them to drink at all in the first place. Turning twenty-one doesn't mean you should drink. It means you can drink—if you have first considered your circumstances and the people around you to see if it is a good idea. Many adults, including many Christians, make a thoughtful and disciplined decision not to drink at all.

Lastly, the Bible has something to say about underage drinking in the United States. God tells us to obey all civil laws unless they prevent us from worshipping him (Romans 13:1-7). Since God puts governments in place, we need to obey the government. So if you break the law by drinking as a teenager, you are also disobeying God.

THE DANGERS OF DRUNKENNESS

Why is being drunk so dangerous? Alcohol is what is called a depressant. That doesn't mean it makes you sad (although that can be a side effect for some people); it means it temporarily slows down your brain.

When you drink too much, your judgment will be compromised. You may take dangerous risks that you normally would have the good sense to avoid. You may pass out or throw up. If you throw up and choke on your vomit after you have passed out or if you get alcohol poisoning, you can even die.

Combining drinking with driving can also be deadly, even if you or the driver are not drunk. Alcohol slows reactions and impairs judgment, and even a slightly delayed reaction in a car traveling 40 mph can be fatal. Car accidents are the #1 killer of teens, and many of them involve alcohol. Never drink and drive, and never ride with someone under the influence of alcohol.

We suggest that you and your parents make a plan ahead of time. If you are in a situation where you or your friends have been drinking, call your parent(s)—they will pick you up, no matter the time or circumstances.

If you get drunk, the morning after you will be greeted with a hangover. You will have a terrible headache and upset stomach and will feel dehydrated, tired, gross, and grumpy.

In addition to those risks, some people become alcoholics. Alcoholism is a disease in which your body must have alcohol. If you know that alcoholism runs in your family, you may be predisposed to be an alcoholic, so it might be a good idea to avoid drinking altogether. Ask your parents if any blood relative in your family is an alcoholic.

So, if these are the risks of drinking too much, why does anyone drink? Here are some reasons.

1. Drinking relaxes you. But eventually, relying on alcohol to relax keeps you from learning to handle relationships with people, or stressful situations, on your own.
2. Drinking lowers your guard. You become more impulsive when you are drinking. You may find it easier to start a conversation with a girl, but you are also more likely to say something stupid or offensive to her. You are more likely to try drugs if you have been drinking.
3. Drinking makes teenagers feel more grown up. It's normal during adolescence to see yourself as more of an adult, and it's natural to want to experience grown-up things. You

see adults sipping wine in restaurants, and you want to experience those adult things too. But alcohol affects you differently than it affects them; we'll talk about that soon.

There are also some medical reasons for an adult to drink. Some doctors encourage adults with certain types of heart problems to drink a glass of red wine several times a week.

THE DIFFERENCE BETWEEN ADULTS AND TEENS DRINKING ALCOHOL

As a teenager, your brain is still forming neural connections, and the part of your brain that handles judgment and decisions is far from being fully developed. That means that you are more impulsive as a teenager than as an adult. Recent studies compared brain scans from young adults who drank as teenagers with the brains of adults who did not, and they show noticeable differences in the development and health of the brain. For the full and healthy development of your brain, it is wise to not drink as a teenager.

So what does this difference between an adult and a teenager consuming alcohol look like? Imagine one of your best friends has a go-cart and a big backyard. The two of you love to ride that go-cart around all over his yard. Of course, you drive it as fast as it will go. You zip around trees and make sharp turns. You love the speed, the wind blowing in your hair, and the power of the engine.

Now pretend for a moment that you and your friend wish the go-cart would go faster, so the two of you secretly take it down to the local BMW dealership and ask the manager to install a V-12, 300 horsepower engine—the same engine found in many BMW's.

Picture the little go-cart with all of the power of that enormous engine. Think how fast you could accelerate from 0-60 miles per hour. Could you go 100 mph? 180 mph? Of course, you tell yourself, we will drive safely. So you and your buddy sneak the suped-up go-cart to his house and, when his mom isn't looking, you crank the engine.

What do you think would happen to you and your friend?

You would barely touch the accelerator, and it would go so fast that you would lose control and flip it. Or maybe you would start out okay for just a little while, but when you hit that first curve, it would go flying because it would be going faster than the aerodynamics or structure of the car could handle. Or maybe when you were ready to stop the go-cart near the garage, you would be going too fast, and the breaks would be too flimsy to stop the little go-cart short of the brick wall.

With the temptation of a powerful engine and the freedom from a parent watching, what boy or teenager would have the self-control and self-discipline to drive the go-cart slowly enough to be safe?

Now this same V-12, 300 horsepower engine is usually very safe in a BMW driven by a responsible adult, but it is dangerous if placed in a smaller vehicle like a go-cart.

As a teenager, you are a go-cart, and putting alcohol in your body is like putting a V-12 engine in a go-cart. It's a formula for disaster. When you are twenty-one or older, you will be much more like a car that is designed to safely fit a V-12 engine in most situations.

Wanting to feel good or wanting to forget about horrible things—that's understandable. But drinking or doing drugs won't make you happy. They won't fix your problems.

What will help with things are going wrong? God. Sometimes, people go to alcohol or drugs because they are trying to hold their life together without God. If you are desperate to feel good, to forget about your problems, or to be liked, ask God for help. He already loves you more than you can imagine, and he can give you joy. He can help you face up to your problems like a man, instead of hiding behind alcohol or drugs.

What are the differences between your parents having a beer or glass of wine and you drinking one?

_____

_____

_____

What exactly will you say or do when someone hands you a beer?

_____

_____

_____

QUESTIONS

SMOKING AND VAPING

You won't just be tempted with alcohol. Tobacco is an early and common teenage temptation. You may think that smoking a cigarette or cigar, or dipping or chewing (putting tobacco in your cheek or gums), isn't a big deal. Most teenage boys underestimate the dangers of tobacco and vaping.

Tobacco leaves and vaping contain a drug called nicotine, which is absorbed into the bloodstream. While many teens think smoking or vaping relaxes you, the nicotine raises your heartbeat and blood pressure and causes the release of a hormone that creates physiological stress.

Nicotine is as addictive as heroin or cocaine—once you start using it, you may not ever be able to quit. Also, once you start, your body gets used to the chemical effect, so you eventually need more and more nicotine to feel the same impact that your body now intensely craves.

When your body doesn't have the nicotine it is addicted to, it makes you irritable, anxious, tired, and nauseated, as well as giving you headaches and trouble sleeping. That sounds miserable. So why do people smoke or vape?

» Peer pressure plays a factor. You want to fit in.
» Some smoke because they are stressed and think it will relax them.
» Some smoke because it's a way to show they aren't kids anymore, or because they want to rebel against their parents.
» Some are just bored and see it as something adventurous to do.

The good news is that if you can resist the pressure to smoke for just a few years, you will almost certainly never smoke. About 90% of smokers began smoking as a teenager.[7] Adults rarely start smoking; most started as teenagers and have not been able to quit, even though nearly all of them want to quit. It is easier never to start than it is to stop.

DRUGS

Teenagers abuse a variety of drugs, both legal and illegal. Common legally available drugs:

» **Painkillers** are prescribed for pain and are only legally available by prescription. Painkiller abuse can be dangerous and even deadly with too high a dose, or when taken with other drugs, like alcohol. Some painkillers can be addictive, especially opioids (there's more about those in the section about illegal drugs). Brand names include Vicodin, Tylenol with Codeine, OxyContin, and Percocet.

» **Depressants,** or downers, are prescribed to treat anxiety and panic attacks, tension, severe stress reactions, and sleep disorders. Brand names include Klonopin, Nembutal, Soma, Ambien, Valium, and Xanax.

» **Inhalants** are fumes from glues, aerosols, and solvents. Many teenagers assume that inhaling (breathing in) common household items can't be a big deal, so they sniff things from cans or bags, or soak rags in them and put the rags in their mouths. These include things like glue, paint thinner, hairspray, spray paints, cleaning fluids, and gasoline. While it may cause temporary happiness and confusion, the toxins can cause headaches, loss of hearing and smell, and sometimes immediate death.

The most commonly used illegal drugs:

» **Marijuana (pot or weed)** is usually smoked in a joint. Marijuana affects your mood, coordination, sense of time, and short-term memory. A lot of teenagers use marijuana because it may provide a temporary good feeling and make it easier to escape some of their stress.

» **Stimulants (cocaine, crack, and speed)** are a powder from the dried leaves of the plant coca. When heated, it crackles and is called crack. Cocaine is snorted, while crack is smoked. Cocaine is a stimulant that shocks the central nervous system and thus produces a 15 to 30-minute intense high and feeling of power. It also can cause the individual to stop breathing or have a heart attack. It is intensely addictive.

» **Opioids** are a group of drugs that include the illegal drug heroin, as well as certain strong painkillers that can be prescribed by doctors. When guys get seriously injured or have surgery, a doctor might prescribe an opioid to help with pain. These drugs help with the pain during recovery, but many people become addicted to them and need them even after the pain is gone. Sometimes people even fake injuries or act like they are in pain to get these painkillers, or they switch from prescribed medications to other kinds of opioids, like heroin. Sometimes people use synthetic opioids like fentanyl. Fentanyl is 80 times stronger than morphine—just a tiny bit can make you overdose.[8] And since fentanyl is cheaper than other opioids, other drugs are increasingly laced with fentanyl, making it very easy to dangerously overdose. Almost half of drug overdose deaths in America involve fentanyl.[9]

» **LSD (acid or doses)** is usually licked off a small square of paper and is a colorless and odorless chemical that changes your mood and makes you hallucinate. Users also experience panic attacks and frightening delusions, and demonstrate very unpredictable behavior, as well as convulsions, an increased heart rate, and even coma.

» **Ecstasy** is a drug produced by underground chemists and is available at parties, concerts, and dance clubs. Usually found in the form of a powder, tablet, or capsule, ecstasy is swallowed or snorted. It is a hallucinogenic and a stimulant that makes emotions very intense. Users may experience tingly skin, depression, paranoia, and a raised body temperature which can damage organs.

The use of illegal drugs is increasing, especially among young teens. But illegal drugs are dangerous—they are chemicals that change how the body works. Your bloodstream carries these chemicals throughout the body, including to the brain. Depending on the drug, the amount taken, and other factors, drugs may deaden or intensify your senses, change your alertness, alter your perceptions, and lessen physical pain. They also shock your brain, heart, and organs and can cause permanent damage or instant death. They are almost always addictive, often from just a first-time use.

STEROIDS

Steroids have been in the news a lot lately with professional athletes. They are made from the male sex hormone testosterone. They increase your body's ability to strengthen its muscles when working out, but they also cause a host of problems:

» Premature balding or hair loss
» Mood swings, including anger, aggression, and depression
» Beliefs that aren't true (delusions) and feelings of mistrust or fear (paranoia)
» Problems sleeping
» Dizziness, nausea, and vomiting
» Greater chance of injuring muscles and tendons
» Liver damage and urinary problems
» Shortening of final adult height
» Increased risk of developing heart disease, stroke and some types of cancer

A lot of guys tell themselves they'll only use steroids for a season or a school year. Unfortunately, steroids can be addictive, making it hard to stop taking them. The consequences are so severe that professional sports leagues have banned them, but most steroid use in this country is during the high school years.

At some point, each of you will see—and have the opportunity to use—alcohol and other drugs. Sadly, the use of alcohol and other drugs occurs among many middle and high school students around the United States, and sometimes even among elementary school students. Boys from all backgrounds can use, and get addicted to, drugs and alcohol.

PLAN AHEAD TO PROTECT YOURSELF

What can you do to protect yourself from making poor and unhealthy decisions about drinking and drugs?

First of all, decide now to not drink, smoke, or use drugs. If you wait to make your decision until you are at a party, you will make the wrong decision. That's a guarantee. Instead, make your decision ahead of time, based on a long-term perspective and based on what God says about drinking and drugs.

Plan what you will say and do when confronted with the opportunity. If you don't have the confidence to say "no way" and walk away, here are some other things you can say:

» "I'll get busted. My mom will smell it on my breath. She said she is going to smell my breath and clothes when I come home."

» "My parents won't let me play on the basketball team if I drink or smoke, and they'll find out. Parents always eventually hear what happens at a party."

» "I don't get my driver's license if I drink or smoke. I'd rather drive as a junior and senior than drink a beer tonight."

Second, avoid putting yourself in situations where sin is likely to win out. Proverbs 1:15 says not to set your foot on the paths of sinners who can entice you. So if you know that there will be drinking and drug use at a party, don't go. If you know that your buddy's parents are out of town and that their liquor cabinet is stocked, don't spend the night at his house. If you know a particular friend is very persuasive and is making poor choices, don't hang out with him on Friday nights. You will probably find that it's easier to say no to the invitation than it is to say no to a beer or joint once you're there.

Finally, know that drinking and using drugs doesn't make you a man. It's not something you have to do to prove your maturity. In fact, it shows a lack of maturity. And it's not an adventure—instead, drinking or doing drugs can hold you back from real adventures. God designed us to enjoy adventure with Him. Following Jesus and fulfilling His mission is the greatest adventure you can ever partake in. Don't believe the lie that the Christian life is boring. Team up with the other boys you know who are following Christ and have wholesome fun together.

In what situations are you most likely to encounter alcohol, cigarettes, and other drugs? Is it worth putting yourself in that situation?

_____

_____

_____

What can you be doing to have noble, helpful adventures so that you aren't looking for fake adventures with alcohol and other drugs?

_____

_____

_____

QUESTIONS

NOTES ON THE DANGERS OF ALCOHOL AND DRUGS

Summarize the most important things you've learned.

_____

_____

_____

_____

_____

_____

_____

_____

_____

_____

Memorize and explain the key verse: Ephesians 5:18.

_____

_____

_____

CHAPTER 07

Relationships and Dating
(The Chapter About Girls!)

My boyfriend used to ask his mother, 'How can I find the right woman for me?' and she would answer, 'Don't worry about finding the right woman—concentrate on becoming the right man.'

Girl, Age 21

Before we start talking about what to do when you start dating, here's one thing not to do: use horrible pick-up lines. You know the ones we're talking about:

» Are you Google? Because you have everything I'm searching for.
» Are you an angel? Because you look like you fell from Heaven.

Whatever you do when you start dating, don't use cheesy pick-up lines. Believe it or not, sometimes the best way to get a girl's attention is to simply be kind to her.

Over the next few years, you will become increasingly interested in girls. They will stir strong feelings in you—both positive and negative. They will make you happy, excited, and eager to be around them. And they will sometimes disappoint you and hurt your heart, especially when a girl lets you know she doesn't feel the same way about you that you feel about her.

God built you to be attracted to girls and women. So the attraction that you feel—or will increasingly feel—is a wonderful and natural thing. At this point in your life, you may or may not be interested in girls, and that's fine. Some of you are more comfortable talking with and about girls than others are, and that's fine too.

There is no magical age or moment when you are suddenly supposed to be interested in girls. A lot of guys feel a pressure or expectation to have a girlfriend or date in middle school or high school, and that can cause a lot of anxiety. But like other things in our lives, liking girls and being ready to date unfolds at different times for different people.

Don't fake an interest in girls before you feel an interest in them, and don't begin dating and forming serious relationships before you are ready for them. There is nothing wrong with not dating in middle school and high school. It doesn't mean you won't have a girlfriend or get married later. In fact, it's often a sign of maturity.

One thing to consider is that dating someone at an early age could hurt or damage a friendship that could last for a long time. It is healthy and natural to have a desire to get know girls. But get to know them as friends first, so that you are more prepared to have a relationship as you get older. Don't sacrifice friendships with girls just so that you can say you have a girlfriend.

Don't be in a rush to be girl-crazy or to date or have a girlfriend. Boy-girl relationships can be complicated—they can have painful real-life consequences, especially if you aren't ready for them. In fact, we would suggest that you wait to date. Though it can be exciting to think about being in a relationship with a girl, at your age, the potential dangers are greater than the possible benefits.

The concept of dating is actually not even present in the Bible. The only time a young man and woman entered into a relationship was when they were preparing for marriage. As the quote at the beginning of the chapter suggests, at this stage in your life, we think you ought to focus on becoming the right man, not on finding the right girl.

WHY WAIT TO DATE?

1. Dating means the risk of rejection. You might hear or say something like, "No, I don't want to date you," or "I like someone else better than you." It hurts deeply to be told that, especially when you really like the person. Rather than run the risk of rejection, realize that no one really knows what they want or who they like at this stage in life. In junior high, attraction to someone of the opposite sex is usually very fickle and shallow. Give yourself time to develop into a man who is secure enough in who he is in Christ that he can recover from of rejection.

2. Boy-girl relationships can make you try to be someone you are not. We invent personalities for ourselves. We become actors—people we are not—in an effort to impress girls, to be the sort of person we think they want us to be, and to be cool. It takes a lot of energy and thought to reinvent ourselves; it's draining. It can lead to confusion and doubts about who we really are. And ultimately, it disappoints God, who chose to make you the way you are. At your age, you need to focus on learning who God made you to be, not on who you think a girl wants you to be.

3. Boy-girl relationships involve powerful emotions. Teenage boys, no matter how smart they are, do not yet have the life experiences to fully understand love and act out love for a girl. Teenagers, and even adults, often confuse crushes and infatuation (an attraction based on superficial things) and lust (an attraction based on sexual desire) for love. It's like thinking that you can fly an airplane just because you have a driver's license for a car. You'll crash if you try to operate something too complicated (like love or an airplane) before you fully understand how it works. And a relationship crash can have very significant consequences.

4. Boy-girl relationships are potentially dangerous because they can tempt you to make poor choices that are displeasing to God and can have life-altering consequences. The changes in your bodies (which we will discuss in the next chapter) produce strong urges to engage in sexual activities with girls. And much of our society—movies, TV, many adults, some of your friends—will say that sexual activity outside of marriage is okay. The girl you really like, or that you think you love, may also say it is okay. But none of

those voices change God's design for sexual activity as something that happens within the safe bounds of marriage.

There are other reasons that boy-girl relationships during the teenage years can be potentially dangerous, but these are some important ones. So what do you do? Just stay away from girls? No. Instead, one of the most important things you can do is to have a proper view of girls and relationships:

» Girls are children of God, created, like you, in his image.
» Girls should be treated with respect and kindness.

Take your time getting to know girls. Get to know them in a safe and comfortable environment. Go on group dates. Hanging out with a bunch of girls and guys is usually a safe and fun way to spend time with girls.

As you become more interested in girls, it can be easy to start thinking about them only as potential dates. But it's important to remember that girls can be great friends. When you start as friends, you will both be more yourselves, and you will get to know each other more honestly and comfortably.

WHEN AM I READY TO DATE?

A successful relationship of any sort takes work. Just feeling strong attraction—even feeling love—is not enough. Relationships are based on serving one another: putting her needs in front of your needs, sacrificing what you may want, doing thoughtful and unexpected things for her.

One-on-one dating in middle school is not necessary, and it's usually not a good idea. Too many things can go wrong, which can endanger your ability to have the better experiences waiting for you down the road.

By the way, many boys in middle school who say they have a girlfriend have one in name only. They usually don't actually go out on dates, see each other, or even talk all that much. In middle school in particular, boys usually just have a girlfriend to look cool.

Do you want to know what you can be doing to become the right man? Below is a list of actions that ought to be a normal part of your life before you are ready to date. We would suggest holding off on dating until your life looks like this and your parents and mentors think you are ready to date.

» Wait until your relationship with God is in a healthy place.

» Wait until you have close friends around you who are committed to helping you live out the Christian life.

» Wait until you can take care of yourself and are responsible.

» Wait until your parents and mentors affirm that you are living out the 7 Virtues of Manhood.

» Wait to date until you have decided what sort of girl you want to date—standards based on how she acts and what she cares about, not just how she looks.

» Wait until you have committed yourself to not engaging in sexual activity outside of marriage.

» Wait until you are mature enough to treat a girl as a sister in Christ. In the meantime, enjoy girls as friends, hang out in groups and get to know them.

Why do you think God created men and women differently?

_____

_____

What does God say about how we are to think about girls? When you think about girls, what goes through your mind?

_____

_____

What are the right reasons to date and be in a relationship with a girl?

_____

_____

QUESTIONS

WHOM SHOULD I DATE?

When you get older, and are ready to date, how will you know whom to ask out? How can you know if a girl will break your heart? You can't protect yourself from every heartbreak, but you can avoid some painful mistakes if you choose your date wisely. After you've spent time for the next several years becoming the right man, here are some things to think about before you ask a girl out:

Is she a friend or a stranger? This seems like a no-brainer, but it is better to know someone before you ask her out. Asking someone you don't know at all can work out, but it is risky. Date someone whom you have known for a while—that way, you know what she is all about.

Does she respect others? Pay close attention to how the girl you are interested in treats your peers and other people. If she is kind and respectful to others, she will probably be that way with you as well.

Is she headed in the same direction? Dating can be difficult with someone who doesn't believe in the same things that you do. Is she obviously a committed Christian? The girl you choose to date one day should be way more interested in Jesus than she is in you.

Does she keep her word? Ask yourself if this person keeps her commitments in other areas of her life. You want to look for someone who keeps her promises—otherwise, you could set yourself up for a painful betrayal.

One day, when you are ready to date, here are some ways to date well:

- » Show extra-good manners around girls. A polite young man should:
  - » Walk ahead of his date in a darkened theater or room.
  - » Walk on the side of the sidewalk that is closer to the road.
  - » Stand when a girl the same age or a woman enters the room and stand when she leaves.
  - » Wait until the women have been seated (and help them be seated if it is a formal date) before seating himself.
  - » Don't start eating before his date.
  - » Always thank a girl after a dance or date.
  - » Open car and building doors as a sign of respect.
- » Speak respectfully of all girls. The way you talk about people is a reflection of whether you value you them as God does. Also, if you develop a reputation for treating any girl poorly or

saying inappropriate things about even one girl, we can almost assure you that many girls will hear about it.

» Take the initiative and lead in the relationship. God charges men to take the first step to serve and lead, and girls usually like that. Ask them out, and make sure to ask a while before the date night. Suggest the plans for what you will do on the date. Of course, you should look for things you think she will like and be willing to change your plans, but take the responsibility to come up with the ideas.

» Take the lead in establishing the boundaries, intensity, and pace of your relationship and talking about your relationship. That's your role—don't neglect it, even if the girl is more assertive in driving the relationship.

» Go slowly with your relationship. Good relationships are marathons, not sprints, and many relationships start out too quickly and intensely to last. You can't run a marathon at full speed. In the early stages of the relationship, resist the urge to talk every single day, to see each other at every opportunity, and to kiss and say "I love you" too soon. Your relationship will be much more likely to survive and thrive.

» Respect her future. Remember that you are with someone's future wife. You do not want to do anything that would damage her future relationships. And remember that she is made in the image of God, just like you, and she is precious to God, just like you. Messing with a girl's emotions or pressuring her to cross boundaries can hurt her. As a husband someday, you'll be called to reflect Jesus' love for your wife by how you love and protect her. Start practicing that now by caring for and protecting the girls you date.

KISSING

Kissing is great. It feels really good. It's exciting (and nerve-racking at first). But you should understand that kissing is meant to lead to sex—it wasn't meant to be a stopping point.

So you need to show discipline and restraint in how you kiss, where you kiss, and how long you kiss. To keep from sliding down the slippery slope to sex, we suggest either not kissing at all or only short kisses—for one second—and kisses on the cheek or with the mouth closed. Long kisses and open-mouthed kisses fire up your sexual engines, making you want to touch more of a girl's body. Kisses on a sofa or away from anyone else are also more dangerous than a kiss at the front door. Because of these dangers, some people wait to kiss until they are engaged or married.

Save your first kiss. Don't give your first kiss away quickly or cheaply. At the wrong time, kissing can mess things up. All of a sudden, when you kiss a girl, it signifies you are more than friends. Both you and she may not be ready for all the new pressures, expectations, and roles that come with that. It may make things awkward. A lot of good friendships get short-circuited by a kiss too soon. Kissing is personal and private and most appropriately done when someone is actually your girlfriend (or someday, your wife). Wait on kissing for a while.

Kissing is one of the benefits and privileges of marriage. It should not be taken lightly. Don't try to enjoy the benefits of marriage before you are ready for the responsibilities also.

INFATUATION VS. LOVE

How do you know if you really like this girl or even love her? Here's how you can tell the difference:

Infatuation is often short-lived and based on superficial things because you don't know the girl very well. An infatuation is like when a new video game comes out. It's cool for a while, but then you lose interest in it and want something newer. You may go through several infatuations in the next few years.

Lust is an attraction based only on physical attributes that stir up physical desires and responses in you. Guard yourself against lust.

Love, on the other hand, is a deep, complex, and mature emotion and set of actions. When do I know I love someone? When do I tell her I love her? Both are very difficult questions to answer. Don't say "I love you" until you know what it means and how it will change your relationship. Love is not just a feeling—those three words mean sacrifice and service, commitment, and protection.

Ask yourself this question on a regular basis: do I love her, do I love it that she loves me, or do I love being in love? Those are three very different things. The last two are not love. While they may feel good, they are shallow and selfish. They show that you do not yet have a mature enough understanding of love.

Love is patient, love is kind. It does not envy, it does not boast, it is not proud. It does not dishonor others, it is not self-seeking, it is not easily angered, it keeps no record of wrongs. Love does not delight in evil but rejoices with the truth. It always protects, always trusts, always hopes, always perseveres.

1 CORINTHIANS 13:4-7

NAVIGATING RELATIONSHIPS IN A GOD-GLORIFYING WAY

As we end this chapter, here is some practical advice on how to navigate dating and relationships in a way that is healthy and glorifying to God:

» Make sure you are maintaining balance in your life. Girlfriends can tip your life out of balance. It's easy to invest a lot of time, emotions, and energy in a girl. Your grades, activities, and other relationships can slip, but you will likely have a blind-spot to this. So ask your parents and friends if they see an imbalance that needs to be corrected. Also, be careful not to damage your friendships by neglecting your buddies and spending too much time with your girlfriend.

» Respect your parents' rules and boundaries. We'll talk about parents in a later chapter, but for now, know that they have more wisdom than you do. Their rules and boundaries are probably wise ones that will benefit you. Seek their advice about girls. Another good idea: practice treating your mom the way you would a date— hold doors for her and use your best manners.

» Go out of your way to gain the respect of your date's parents. Get to know them. Be honest with them. Don't put on an act to get them to like you. Ask them if you can take their daughter out on a date. This sounds old-fashioned, but it's essential. A girl's parents can practically make or break your relationship. They will have a big influence on how their daughter thinks about you.

» Learn about the needs and preferences of girls. As you get older, you'll realize that men and women have some important differences. If you try to relate to girls the way you do to boys, you'll have a difficult time with your relationships.

WHAT GIRLS WANT YOU TO KNOW

This book was written at a school for boys, and every year we invite some godly high school girls to share what they wish guys knew. Here are some of their tips:

» Listening is better than fixing. When a girl feels emotional or has a problem, she may not be ready to fix it. She may just want to talk about it and feel understood. Friendship really matters. Some girls get frustrated that guys don't seem to be interested in friendship if there's not a shot at something more.

» Real Christian men respect women. Guys sometimes get the idea that it's okay to talk badly about girls when they're not around—to make comments about their bodies or to mock them for their moods. That is always, always wrong.

» Looks do matter, but not as much as what's inside. Women want to be with men they can respect for their strength, integrity, and commitment.

» Date other believers. The Bible instructs Christians to marry fellow believers. A fellow believer can—and should—encourage your walk with the Lord. A romantic relationship with someone with a different set of beliefs is like juggling dynamite.

» "Put me second." Christian girls are looking for a guy who has made God number one in his life above everything, including them.

» Break up respectfully. It is unlikely that you will marry anyone you date as a teenager, so teenage relationships will probably involve a breakup. Breakups usually involve some pain for at least one person, so they should be done with care, compassion, and respect. Break up in person—never by email, in a text message, or through someone else. Remember that the girl you are dating is precious to God and also probably someone's future wife, so you should respect her and her future husband by how you treat, protect, and break up with her.

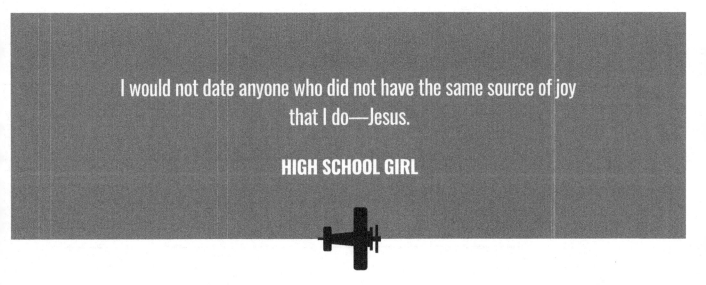

I would not date anyone who did not have the same source of joy that I do—Jesus.

HIGH SCHOOL GIRL

Developing meaningful relationships with girls is a great adventure. There will be ups and downs, but holding a biblical perspective on girls and relationships can even out the bumps of the next few years.

What are the characteristics of a girl you would like to date?

_____

_____

_____

_____

_____

What do you think are the key ingredients of a good dating relationship?

_____

_____

_____

_____

_____

QUESTIONS

Summarize the most important things you've learned.

_____

_____

_____

_____

_____

_____

_____

_____

_____

_____

Memorize and explain the key verse: 1 Corinthians 13:4-5.

_____

_____

_____

NOTES ON RELATIONSHIPS AND DATING

CHAPTER 08

Understanding Puberty

Becoming a man means your body is going to start changing, but do not be alarmed or think it is only happening to you, because it is happening to your friends too.

Thomas, Age 14

Fighter pilots fly high-performance jets in combat. Their primary job is to defend our troops and positions against attacks by enemy aircraft.

To become a fighter pilot, you first must join the Air Force or the Navy—the only branches of the U.S. military to use fighter planes. All pilots in both the United States Air Force and Navy are commissioned officers, and the first requirement for being an officer is to be a college graduate. But fighter pilots must also meet the physical, psychological, and intellectual requirements before they can even start their training.

These tests are grueling. Potential pilots go through intense physical training. Their eyes are checked; their math skills are tested; their backgrounds are researched. They are pummelled with g-forces (the feeling of pressure you experience at high speeds, like in a roller coaster) up to eight times the intensity of gravity, strong enough to drive the blood out of their brains.

The next few years of your life will be a physical and psychological test for you, preparing you to be a godly man. This chapter is critical to helping you go through the next stage of your life. At some point in the near future, you will begin the adventurous yet potentially dangerous transition from being a boy to becoming a man.

Many things will begin to change, if they have not already. Perhaps the most noticeable change will be your body. Eventually, you will see how these changes in your body and your interest in girls will fit together one day as part of God's great plan for you as a man. Let's start by looking at this time when your body undergoes its most significant transformation since you were a baby. This phase of life is often called puberty.

WHAT IS PUBERTY?

Puberty is a time in each person's life when his or her body starts changing from a child body to an adult body. It's a time of rapid and intense physical changes. It can be a confusing and sometimes uncomfortable process, even for people who seem so secure and happy on the outside.

The biological changes not only impact your body, but they affect your thoughts and emotions as well. Every boy should know what to expect in the upcoming years, why it is happening, and how it is a part of God's plan. Knowing this and remembering that it's normal and natural can help you feel less uncomfortable as a teenager.

Let's look at what actually happens during puberty.

QUESTIONS BOYS ASK ABOUT PUBERTY:

> » When will I get muscles?
> » What's up with body hair?
> » Do I think about girls too much or not enough?
> » Why do I smell?

Around your age, the pituitary gland in your brain will send a message to your testicles to start making a hormone called testosterone. A hormone is a chemical that your body uses like a messenger, sending it to different body parts to tell them what to do next. This testosterone will go from your testicles and travel through your blood throughout your whole body. (If you were a girl, your body would make two different chemicals, estrogen and progesterone, in the ovaries instead of the testicles).

This testosterone makes your body do a few things:

> » Your voice gets deeper.
> » You grow to pretty much your full height. As you grow, you may be somewhat clumsy until you get used to your new size. And your joints will sometimes ache.
> » Your skin becomes oilier, causing pimples. Sometimes, no matter how many times you wash your face or how much cream you put on, you may have some acne.
> » You start to grow hair under your arms and on your face, beginning with the mustache area, chin, and sideburns. This usually happens somewhat later. (By the way, don't be in a rush to shave. It's a pain).
> » Your sweat glands begin working—it would probably be a good idea to start using deodorant now if you aren't yet.
> » Your muscles and strength increase.
> » Your penis and testicles get bigger.
> » You develop pubic hair around your groin and testicles. The hair helps keep the testicles warm enough to produce sperm. (We're about to get to that).
> » Your testicles start to make semen and produce millions of sperm. Semen is a fluid containing sperm, which enables you to produce a child with a woman.
> » You have the ability to ejaculate, which is when your erect penis shoots out semen and its sperm.
> » You will begin having frequent and strong sexual feelings, sometimes when you least expect or want to. This will sometimes involve having erections at both expected and unexpected times, occasionally having wet dreams at night, and feeling the urge to masturbate. (We'll talk about wet dreams and masturbation later in the next chapter)

Don't be ashamed or embarrassed by this. It's God's handiwork. Let's take a look at what God is up to with puberty.

Here are God's three key purposes for puberty:

- » God wants us to grow into men, with grown-up capabilities.
- » God wants us to be able to have the children he may bless us with.
- » God wants us to lead joyful and pleasurable lives.

These changes might feel scary, but they lead to great things. Puberty is not something we control. You may have already begun puberty, or it might start in a few months or years. Either way, when you start puberty has nothing to do with how much of a man you will be in the end or how much respect you're worthy of. So relax—it will happen to you exactly when God wants it to.

One other thing: puberty is not something to be laughed at. You are making fun of God's handiwork and God himself, since we were all created in his image. Don't make fun of anyone for his or her stage of puberty, whether they are entering it a bit earlier or a bit later.

PUBERTY AND SEX

How does puberty relate to sex, and what exactly is sex?

A lot of puberty relates to sex. Sex is not a dirty word, and it should not be a mysterious word. God created sex for us to enjoy, but there is a lot of false information about sex. If most of what you know about sex comes from TV, movies, or the internet, then you will have a narrow view of sex and women, and you are at risk for making unhealthy and damaging choices. And if most of what you know about sex comes from your friends or an older sibling, then you probably don't have all the facts.

It is important that you understand the biology of sex, but it's even more important that you have a biblical understanding of sex. God has a lot to say about sex. One entire book of the Bible, Song of Solomon, centers on courtship, engagement, wedding, marriage, sexual attraction, and the fulfillment that a man and woman share. The book talks about his longing for her, the beauty of her body, and even sex on their wedding night. As men, we are made to see the beauty of women and feel passion and longing for them. We are made even to crave to be intimate with them, to want to have sex with them.

As this entire book of the Bible illustrates, sex is a beautiful act God created for a husband and wife to enjoy. Many married couples have sex multiple times a week because it is so special and powerful. It is an act of passion, intimacy, joy, and procreation.

When a husband and wife have sex, it is a very intimate act, exposing their emotions, vulnerabilities, and hopes. It involves the whole being—not just a body part. It is a spiritual act of marriage, created and blessed by God to bring a husband and wife closer.

However, it's still important to understand its physical nature. Sexual intercourse is the main act of sex. The Bible describes sexual intercourse as when two people become one flesh (Genesis 2:24). We suggest you ask your dad or mentor for more information on what intercourse is.

Before puberty, your testicles do not produce the semen and sperm necessary to conceive a child. Now, at puberty, you are physically and biologically able to father a child. In addition, the testosterone now racing through your body will make you want to do this. You will experience these sexual urges and thoughts you have never felt before. It might be when you see a specific girl or think about a woman you saw in a movie; it may be in math class or in the middle of the night or when you wake up in the morning. As the testosterone stirs these sexual impulses, blood rushes to the tissue in the penis, making it hard. Starting in puberty, this may happen 7-10 times a day or more, as testosterone has 7-10 or more big spurts through the body each day. Don't panic when this happens. It's normal. Remember, God made us the way we are, with testosterone surging through our bodies during adolescence. And in Genesis 1:31, God said he was very pleased with what he made.

Depending on your age, it may seem foreign to you that sex would be appealing. Just thinking about the act of sex seems gross to children. The idea of being naked in front of a girl probably seems impossible and utterly embarrassing. Over the next few years, you will think about sex differently than you do right now.

GOD'S RESTRICTIONS ON SEX (AND WHY HE HAS THEM)

God created sex as a joyful, pleasurable, and intimate act, and he places restrictions on it—not to keep us from enjoying life, but to protect us. His restrictions are acts of love, like parents telling their children not to play in the street or with a loaded gun.

The most important restriction on sex is that God wants you to only have sex in marriage with your wife. God does not permit sex before you are married. He doesn't say, "If you are in love, you may have sex," or "If you have a serious girlfriend, you may have sex," or "If it's a special occasion with a girl, you may have sex." He doesn't say, "Once you are an adult, you may have sex."

He says that sex is only blessed in marriage. And once you are married, you may not have sex with anyone who is not your wife. The Bible is very clear about this. The term for anyone who has sex with someone other than his or her spouse is an "adulterer".

Hebrews 13:4 makes this clear. "Marriage should be honored by all, and the marriage bed kept pure, for God will judge the adulterer and all the sexually immoral." Genesis recounts the experience of Jacob, who loved Rachel, but he waits to have sex with her until he was allowed to marry her. Look at what Jacob said to her father in Genesis 29:21: "Then Jacob said to Laban, 'Give me my wife. My time is completed, and I want to lie with her.'" Notice the order: marriage and then sex. He was obviously very attracted to her. He loved her. But he knew he was supposed to marry her before having sex.

Another story in Genesis also illustrates that God forbids sex outside of marriage. Joseph, as a young man, was working for a man named Potiphar. Potiphar's wife, probably a beautiful woman, attempted to seduce Joseph. She invited him to have sex with her. What did Joseph do? He fled from the room. Joseph knew he should not have sex with a woman who was not his wife.

So what are the Bible's key messages about sex? Here they are:

- » Sex is a gift from God for married couples, and it is only blessed in marriage. We must stay away from sex outside of marriage (Hebrews 13:4; Joseph and Potiphar's wife in Genesis 39:9).
- » Sex is an act of unity (Genesis 2:24; 1 Corinthians 6:15-18).
- » Our bodies are temples for the Holy Spirit, and we are to honor God with our bodies (1 Corinthians 6:19).
- » We will be judged by God for sex outside of marriage (Hebrews 13:4).
- » We are to avoid sexual immorality and control our bodies (1 Thessalonians 4:3, Ephesians 5:3).

Sex is a powerful act, able both to create life and to destroy or derail a life. It's like a fire. If you deliberately and carefully build a fire in a brick fireplace in your home, it adds warmth, comfort, light, beauty, and enjoyment. But if you build the same fire right in the middle of your living room floor, it will burn your whole house down. Only when you place sex in marriage, like a fire in a fireplace, does the true blessing of its intended purpose take place.

Having sex outside of marriage creates a lot of problems—some that show up right away and others that are more long-term. It is a fire that burns and scars you and others. Here are some of those problems:

» It hurts your relationship with God by disobeying him. Disobeying God grieves him and distances you from him. You will feel guilty, ashamed, worried, confused, and just plain dirty.

» You will damage your relationship with the girl with whom you have sex. It's impossible to have a normal and healthy relationship with a girl you are not married to if you have sex with her. Some people think having sex brings two people closer together. If they are married, it does; if they are not married, it will make things awkward and confusing.

» You will emotionally hurt a girl. She will feel guilty, used, cheapened, and betrayed by you. Her self-esteem will be damaged because of what you did with her. God says to love our neighbors as ourselves. As men, we are to protect, nurture, cherish, and serve the girls and women in our lives.

» You will lose respect in the eyes of your peers. You will quickly get a bad reputation. Girls will be less likely to want to be your friend, and that special girl you may want to date may also be far less likely to want to go out with you.

» You will have a harder time figuring out what love is. Love means to nourish and cherish someone else as you would your own body. It protects and provides at all times. (Read 1 Corinthians 13:4-7 to learn more about what love means.) Love is very demanding and complicated, and it involves maturity. Premarital sex confuses the complicated emotion of love, but more than that, it violates what love is. Premarital sex is the very opposite of love. It is impatient and selfish. It does not preserve her sexual purity or yours.

That is why a man leaves his father and mother and is united to his wife,
and they become one flesh.

GENESIS 2:24

» You will disappoint the woman you marry one day because you did not save yourself for her. On your wedding night, it is an incredible gift that you can give your wife if you can tell her that you have saved your sexual purity all of these years for her. You will be blown away by the power of the same gift from her. Exchanging these gifts on your wedding night can be an awesome and tremendous way to start your marriage. On the other hand, if you have sex with a girl who does not turn out to be your wife, you are taking what doesn't belong to you. Her sexual purity and integrity is a gift for her to give to her future husband. Don't rob him and her of that gift.

» You may get sexually transmitted infections (STIs), some of which can last a lifetime or kill you.

» You may become a father before you are ready, and this will alter the course of your life forever. It is difficult and extremely demanding to be a father, even as an adult. Raising children well takes maturity, experience, and a huge investment of time and energy.

Those are some of the reasons why God says to wait for sex until you are married. God loves you and doesn't want these things to happen to you. He wants what is best for you.

What is God's purpose for sex?

_____

_____

QUESTIONS

What is so dangerous about sex outside of marriage?

_____

_____

THE LIES ABOUT SEX

Despite these warnings, many teenage boys have sex anyway. Sometimes they do so because they believe lies about sex. They think, "You aren't really a man until you have sex with a girl. You will feel more like a man when you have had sex." That's a lie. Real men protect women and girls from the damage that sex will do to them. Real men nurture and serve the girls and women in their lives. They don't let their selfish desires and lusts rule the day. They control their bodies.

Satan can easily seduce you with a whole lot of other lies as well. He may whisper that it will provide you with fulfillment and wholeness, which we all want and need. He may tell you that it will bring you and your girlfriend closer together, that you are old enough for sex, that it's okay if you love her, and that the Bible's notions on sex are outdated. You may think that you have the emotional maturity to handle a sexual relationship. You may think it is okay because it seems that so many people are doing it. These are lies.

To protect yourself from these lies, be careful where you get your values and standards. You must make a choice—do you follow God, or do you chase the pleasures and people of a sinful world? What will have more influence on you: the Word of God or the world around you?

Beware of a few snares that can trip you up in the challenge to remain sexually pure until your wedding night:

» Pornography—because you come to view women as sex objects rather than children of God.

» Alcohol and drugs—because they cloud your judgment and remove the naturally healthy inhibitions we have that keep us from sex outside marriage.

» Not reading the Scriptures—because you forget that God commands us very clearly not to have sex outside of marriage.

» The need to be cool—because you will start believing people will respect you for having had sex (when, in actuality, they and you will do just the opposite)

» Not deciding now to not wait until marriage to have sex—because the passions and physical excitement of the moment gather such momentum that you and the girl cannot stop short of sex.

» Putting yourself in a situation where it's too easy to have sex—because if you and a girl end up in the backseat of your car or on the sofa when no one is home, you will probably make a major mistake.

PUBERTY AND EMOTIONS

While most of what we have covered in this chapter has been about the body and sex, puberty and adolescence also have an impact on your emotions. With all the pressures of the teenage years and with all the testosterone surging through your body, you can feel more volatile and angrier than you were as a child. You need to be aware of this, understand anger, and figure out an appropriate way to deal with it.

Anger is what psychologists call a secondary emotion—the real or primary feeling is some other emotion, usually fear or frustration, that then gets expressed in an angry outburst. Many teenage boys get frustrated because they are yearning for independence from their parents and resent guidance from them, yet realize they still need some direction. This creates a tension that the teenage boy may feel but not quite understand. At the same time, the teenage years are full of fears: things like not being popular, being picked on, or not being smart enough. These fears can show up as angry outbursts, sometimes at people or in situations that are unconnected. Parents unfairly become the target of many tantrums.

Besides frustration and fear, the other main emotions expressed as anger are embarrassment and inadequacy. If your mom treats you like a child in front of your friends, or your dad is listening to weird music while he's driving you and your friends to the movies, you may be embarrassed, but you are more likely to lash out at them angrily than to tell them they embarrassed you. Making a bad grade, feeling unsure around girls, not being selected for the music group—all of these things can make you feel inadequate and therefore angry. A sense of loss can also lead to anger, and there are a lot of losses during adolescence: the security of childhood, certain friendships, a predictable body, and sometimes the marriage of your parents. The adolescent years are full of things that can spark angry outbursts, and at the same time, all the testosterone in your body can further fuel your anger.

Understanding what is really happening when you are angry can help you to manage your anger in ways that are more appropriate and healthy. Similarly, it is crucial for you to learn to talk about your emotions rather than waiting until something explodes later. If a boy or man doesn't learn to talk about his emotions and what is really on his heart, his most common way to express emotions may be anger—even if what he is really feeling is hurt, loneliness, or some other feeling that should really be expressed in a different way.

My dear brothers and sisters, take note of this: Everyone should be quick to listen, slow to speak and slow to become angry, because human anger does not produce the righteousness that God desires.

JAMES 1:19-20

When you are angry, it is usually a good idea to take a time-out before you say or do something that will make things worse. We make many of our worst decisions when we're mad. Go exercise or write in a journal. Listen to some music. Walk away from a fight. Pray. Prayer, especially prayer for someone who's made you upset, has a way of softening your heart and melting anger.

Then, when you've calmed down, deal with it helpfully and honestly. And if you need to apologize to a parent, sibling, or friend, do so. You'll feel better.

Between the body and the emotions, puberty gives you a lot of tough situations to deal with. It's a time, more than ever before, when knowing God's love for you—and his design and plans for you—can make a huge difference. When the big picture makes sense, and when you know how it turns out, it's a lot easier to find your way, to smooth out the bumps in the road, and to enjoy the journey. Remember that God designed you carefully, that he has a plan for men, and that he has a plan for you as a fully developed man.

The last time you had an angry outburst, what do you think was really going on with your emotions?

_____

_____

_____

_____

_____

What should you do when you feel angry?

_____

_____

_____

_____

QUESTIONS

Summarize the most important things you've learned.

_____

_____

_____

_____

_____

_____

_____

_____

_____

_____

Memorize and explain the key verse: Genesis 2:24.

_____

_____

_____

NOTES ON UNDERSTANDING PUBERTY

CHAPTER 09

Purity and Porn

I will not let anyone walk through my mind
with their dirty feet.

Mahatma Ghandi, Activist

There is no dignity when the human dimension is
eliminated from the person. In short, the problem with
pornography is not that it shows too much of the person,
but that it shows far too little.

Pope John Paul II

The horrific news from brain research about the enslaving
power of pornography is not the last word. God has the
last word. The Holy Spirit has the greatest power. We are
not mere victims of our eyes and our brains.

John Piper, Pastor & Author

Being an airline pilot can be an exciting and highly rewarding job. However, learning the skills to fly a plane is not an easy task. Most pilots have a four-year college degree, followed by flight school, additional courses to learn about specific aircraft, and many practice flights with an instructor by your side. After about 1,500 hours in the air, you might be able to apply to become a professional pilot.

But it doesn't stop there. To make sure they can focus on flying, pilots must learn to keep themselves clear-headed. They can't drink or use drugs before flying, they can't fly when they are exhausted, and they need to watch out for stress or sickness. They need to keep themselves pure from any distractions that might lead them into danger.

In this chapter, we will continue the conversation about keeping yourself pure as a child of God. It is not an easy task, but like a pilot learning to fly a plane, learning to deal with stress and making safe and wise decisions are essential to avoiding a crash landing. Some of these topics are not easy to discuss. Armed with the facts, we hope you can feel comfortable to discuss them with someone close to you.

WET DREAMS AND MASTURBATION

This sex stuff may seem a long way off. But it will be here before you know it.

There are two other things related to puberty and sex that cause teenage boys a lot of confusion and embarrassment: wet dreams and masturbation. We think it's better to go ahead and give you some perspective on them now.

You will have nocturnal emissions, more commonly called wet dreams. This happens when you release semen while you are sleeping. You will wake up and notice that your underpants are a little wet and sticky. The biological sexual pressures that have been building are released in the form of a wet dream. Don't panic or be embarrassed when this happens. No one but you will probably know about it.

You also will probably feel the urge to masturbate. Masturbation is when you stimulate your penis for several minutes by rubbing and touching it until you have an orgasm (semen comes out of the penis as it does during sex or during a wet dream). During the teenage years, you may frequently feel the urge to masturbate.

People have different thoughts on the topic of masturbation. Some teenage boys worry that masturbation may cause bodily damage or hinder their ability to have sex or children one day. It doesn't. Some teenage boys worry that doing it means something is wrong with them. It doesn't. A teenage boy may worry that he is the only person who does this. He isn't.

Some teenage boys worry that doing this means they are going to hell and that God doesn't love them. That isn't necessarily true either. God's love for you is deeper than your actions, good or bad. People only go to heaven and avoid hell when they trust in Jesus' death on the cross that paid for their bad actions. God does in fact hate the sin of sexual lust, but if you have trusted in Jesus for salvation, you are no longer treated like your sins deserve. God shows his love for us by letting us know that he hates our sin and all of the baggage that can come along with it. Don't let Satan deceive you into believing that because masturbation is common, it is harmless. If you are feeling guilty over this sin, then let this guilt help you more deeply appreciate what Jesus has done by carrying your guilt to the cross for you.

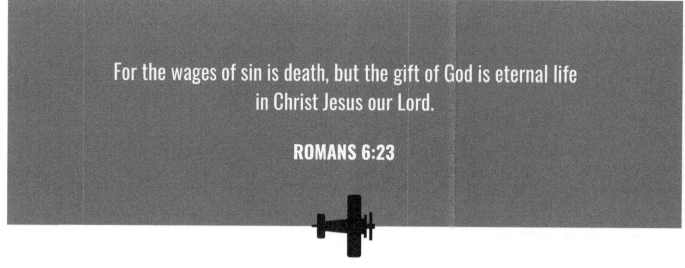

For the wages of sin is death, but the gift of God is eternal life in Christ Jesus our Lord.

ROMANS 6:23

The urge to masturbate is natural for teenage boys, and the temptation is common, yet God calls us to live holy lives. Paul reminds us that the body is always a poor master but can be a useful slave. In other words, don't let your bodily urges control you. Instead, control and use your body in ways that please God.

Here are a few Bible verses to inform your fight against sexual sin:

> » 1 Corinthians 10:13 - No temptation has overtaken you except what is common to mankind. And God is faithful; he will not let you be tempted beyond what you can bear. But when you are tempted, he will also provide a way out so that you can endure it.
> » 2 Timothy 2:20-22 - In a large house there are articles not only of gold and silver, but also of wood and clay; some are for special purposes and some for common use. Those who

cleanse themselves from the latter will be instruments for special purposes, made holy, useful to the Master and prepared to do any good work. Flee the evil desires of youth and pursue righteousness, faith, love and peace, along with those who call on the Lord out of a pure heart.

» 1 Peter 2:11 - Dear friends, I urge you, as foreigners and exiles, to abstain from sinful desires, which wage war against your soul.

Another important topic to cover is oral sex. Some teenagers, including some Christians, may tell you that oral sex is okay because it is not sexual intercourse. We disagree very strongly. Oral sex is sex. God's prohibition against sex outside of marriage includes all sexual acts, not just the act of intercourse.

PORNOGRAPHY

One of the most important fronts in the fight for purity is the fight against pornography. What is pornography? Here is how the Merriam Webster dictionary defines it: "The depiction of erotic behavior (as in pictures or writing) intended to cause sexual excitement." And by "erotic behavior" the dictionary basically means sex or nudity.

You might wonder, "Well, what's the big deal about seeing pictures and videos of naked women? It's not like it's hurting anyone, right?" But what you may not realize is that it's hurting you.

Any impurity, including sexual impurity, keeps you from enjoying closeness with God. He doesn't reject or forsake you, but sin will distance you from him. Hear how James tells us to approach God: "Come near to God and he will come near to you. Wash your hands, you sinners, and purify your hearts, you double-minded" (James 4:8).

PORNOGRAPHY CHANGES THE WAY YOU VIEW WOMEN

You can easily—and often without realizing it—start to view women as body parts or sexual partners.

1. Pornography gives you a wrong impression of how women behave and of what are appropriate boundaries with them.
2. Pornography trains you to relate to women in unholy ways and in ways in which you do not have to share your own emotions and thoughts with them.

PORNOGRAPHY IS ADDICTING

Pornography does not just affect how you relate to women. It is essentially a drug. It is addictive. When you look at sexually explicit images, the same chemical in your brain is being released as if you were snorting cocaine. That's powerful!

Even if you think you'll just look at porn once, you'll probably look at it again and again after that, because your mind will remember and crave those images. And more than that, they can be the fuel that revs up your sexual engine so intensely that you feel a nearly irresistible urge to have sex or to masturbate obsessively.

Like the drugs we discussed a few chapters ago, a lot of teenage boys first look at pornography because of curiosity or maybe because a friend is doing it. They may think it will be an adventure. After all, it's something off limits—the naked female body.

PORNOGRAPHY DOESN'T DELIVER ON ITS PROMISES

A lot of guys are bored or feel an emptiness inside. Boys and men with a hole inside their hearts often rely on a picture or fantasy to provide the love and affirmation they aren't getting elsewhere. But, as with other drugs, pornography leads to more emptiness, deeper shame, and a sense of abandonment and entrapment—things that can keep us from enjoying intimacy and joy with God.

You are becoming today the person you will be as a grown-up man.

Even though our sins are forgiven through Jesus, they still have real-world consequences. They still hurt our minds, bodies, and hearts. The patterns and attitudes you develop as a teenager follow you into adulthood and marriage. You may be more likely to struggle with intimacy with your wife and less likely to experience sexual fulfillment with her. You may carry guilt and images and memories you can't erase. Too many boys make the mistake of thinking that what they do as a teenager doesn't matter in the long run, but you are becoming today the person you will be as a grown-up man.

STANDING GUARD

What can you do to avoid getting drawn into pornography?

1. Recognize its dangers
2. Don't put yourself in situations that will tempt you to look at explicit images
3. Make the decision not to have a computer with internet access, your phone, or a TV in your bedroom
4. Ask your parents to put a filter on your computer and your phone, and ask them to review sites you have visited
5. Have a buddy or mentor hold you accountable for websites you visit and movies you watch

The prudent see danger and take refuge, but the simple keep going and pay the penalty.

PROVERBS 27:12

Temptation is inevitable, so you will need parents, friends, and mentors to help you resist. Even one of the world's most famous and respected preachers, Billy Graham, knew he would be tempted, so he had his assistants go through his hotel room in advance and remove anything, including magazines and pictures on the wall, that could possibly lead him to impure thoughts. They even removed the television. Once, when the hotel room's TV was wired so that it could not be unplugged and removed, he ripped the TV out of the wall and paid for the damage, saying, "I'd rather pay for the damages to this hotel room than let Satan get a stronghold in this battle and allow him to damage my soul." If Billy Graham was presented with temptations, and if Jesus faced worldly temptations in the desert, we can assure you that you'll be tempted also.

God knows how strong these temptations are and that purity doesn't come to us naturally. That's why Paul tells us in 1 Corinthians 6:18 to flee from them. He knows how easily they can trip us up. He knows that even a hint of sexual immorality can harm us (Ephesians 5:3). Let's read each of these verses together.

Flee from sexual immorality. All other sins a person commits are outside the body, but whoever sins sexually, sins against their own body. (1 Corinthians 6:18)

But among you there must not be even a hint of sexual immorality, or of any kind of impurity, or of greed, because these are improper for God's holy people. (Ephesians 5:3)

What do you think these two verses mean for your fight against sexual sin? How can you flee? What does it mean for there to "not be even a hint of sexual immorality" in your life?

WHAT IF I'M ALREADY STRUGGLING?

If you are currently struggling with porn, seek God's forgiveness and help. Ask for him to give you the strength to walk away from it. If you have impure images or thoughts from the past that you can't seem to shake, you may need to be very disciplined in meditating on verses, wholesome songs, and other things to replace the old images or songs. A parent or counselor may also be able to help you. Don't be ashamed to ask for help—many men need help with this.

Address these issues now before they grow into bigger problems. Don't buy into the fake manhood that our culture tries to sell. It's trying to trick you into seeking a false sense of adventure, instead of the authentic, bold adventures that real men should be pursuing. It keeps us from being True Friends because it limits our ability to be open and intimate. We don't protect and serve girls and women as Noble Knights and Servant Leaders should when we are using them to satisfy our lusts.

Most significantly, it turns our hearts away from God as we seek to find our value in something cheap and sinful rather in God's creation and redemption of us. Don't cheat yourself out of authentic manhood and the fullness of joy and fellowship with your Creator.

No temptation has overtaken you except what is common to mankind. And God is faithful; he will not let you be tempted beyond what you can bear. But when you are tempted, he will also provide a way out so that you can endure it.

I CORINTHIANS 10:13

Describe in your own words why pornography is bad for you.

_____

_____

_____

Have you already faced the temptation to look at explicit images? Where were you when you were tempted? What steps are you going to take to protect yourself from that situation in the future?

_____

_____

_____

If you haven't been tempted yet, what steps are you going to take to protect yourself from tempting situations?

_____

_____

_____

QUESTIONS

TEMPTATIONS FROM MEDIA

One of the first attacks on your attempts to stay pure will come from the media. Almost every TV show and movie has something to do with sex, whether through crude jokes, graphic scenes, or sexual relationships between unmarried people. While watching sports on television or scrolling through social media, you will see countless advertisements that focus on sex or suggest that if you wear a certain deodorant or drink a certain alcohol, girls will be all over you. Advertisers know what they are doing. They know what attracts the attention of boys and men.

Be very careful about what you look at and how much time you spend watching TV or exploring the internet. Be careful whom you follow or what you search for on Instagram or Snapchat. And don't try to handle the attacks all on your own—discuss what you see with your parents or a mentor.

Television can have a powerful effect on your beliefs about sex, especially beliefs about marriage and girls. The few studies done indicate that teenagers who get most of their information about sexuality from television will have higher criteria for female beauty and will accept the idea of premarital sex and extramarital intercourse with one or more partners.

UNC CENTER FOR RESEARCH IN JOURNALISM

REMAINING PURE

With temptations all around you, the struggle to keep your heart, mind, and body pure is not easy. It is a battle that too many boys lose.

So how can a teenage boy fight this battle and win? King David asked the same question hundreds of years ago.

How can a young person stay on the path of purity?

By living according to your word.

I seek you with all my heart;

do not let me stray from your commands.

I have hidden your word in my heart

that I might not sin against you. (Psalm 119:9-11)

This passage instructs us to do a few things.

Live according to God's Word. How do you stay pure? By reading, listening to and obeying God's Word.

Seek God and obey his commands. Get to know God personally. Talk with him in prayer. Obey his commands.

Memorize God's Word. Hide God's word in your heart. God's Word needs to be the dominant voice you hear in your head, not the world's.

In addition to these instructions from this verse, here are a few other tips:

Understand God's plan and design, as well as his standards and commands. He designed us with senses so that we might be excited by what we see and touch. He built us to see the beauty of women. He created a sex drive in us. He wants us to experience pleasure within marriage.

Know you are under attack. We all have a sinful nature, and those senses for beauty and pleasure are easily twisted into self-serving, sinful desires. God, being completely holy and desiring a relationship with us, calls us to a standard of perfect purity—purity of thought and action. He wants us to seek him with all our heart, and he wants our hearts to be pure and centered on him.

Understand God's standards are high. No sex outside of marriage. No hint of sexual immorality. No lust. No impure thoughts. Jesus tells us in Matthew 5:28 that looking lustfully at a girl is committing adultery in our hearts. That's a tough standard.

Know that the battle will be difficult. Boys and men face many temptations, but perhaps none is more difficult than our struggle with sexual purity, especially pornography and the many other sins to which it leads. We are visual people. Things we see make a big impact on us (often a bigger impact than they would make on girls who saw them).

Don't fight the battle on your own. The pressure from media is one that you will always fight. It doesn't get any easier. But you don't have to fight this battle alone. You will need guys to fight with you and hold you accountable.

Ask God for help. The most important thing to remember is that we can rely on God's strength and grace in times of difficulty. He is faithful, and he promises us that he will never leave us.

Do you have a friend or mentor who will hold you accountable in your effort to be pure? If not, who would be someone you could ask?

_____

_____

_____

What are you doing to train your mind to think about those things that are pure, noble, and excellent?

_____

_____

_____

QUESTIONS

Summarize the most important things you've learned.

_____

_____

_____

_____

_____

_____

_____

_____

Memorize and explain the key verse: 1 Corinthians 10:13.

_____

_____

_____

NOTES ON PURITY AND PORN

CHAPTER 10
Screens, Stories, and Songs

All television is educational television. The question is: what is it teaching?

Nicholas Johnson, Professor and Former FCC Commissioner

Do you like a good challenge?

In the 1950s, there was a fighter pilot named John Boyd who would challenge any other pilot he could find to a test. If the pilot could knock him down in a combat duel in the flight simulator in 40 seconds or less, Boyd would pay him $40. Pilot after pilot took his challenge, but Boyd never had to pay that $40. He just kept winning.

Boyd's secret to his success was his ability to counter-attack his opponent. He had an answer for every move that a pilot could put on him. "Forty-Second Boyd" will go down in history as one of the best combat pilots this world has ever seen.[11]

You are about to enter a time in your life when your mind will be under attack. Our culture has created a barrage of ways to influence your thinking. You will see and hear things that go against God's Word. Your thinking will be challenged. A lot of things will compete for your time. You must be prepared with countermeasures. This chapter looks at the many ways culture tries to shape your thoughts and actions, so that you can expect its maneuvers and plan how you will counter them.

TRAINING YOUR MIND

If you've ever been on a sports team, you probably the importance of conditioning in playing your best. Push-ups, sprints, drills—these might not look like the final game, but you wouldn't win without them.

But did you know that you need to train your mind just as much as you need to train your body?

Just as your body shows how you train, your mind shows what you see and hear. The movies you watch or the websites you spend time on might not seem to affect how you serve others or love God. But little by little, they can build up spiritual muscles of discernment, empathy, and wisdom—or they can make those muscles grow weak.

Nobody does drills and conditioning by accident. If you want to build up your spiritual muscles, you'll need to work at it. That means taking the time to know God's Word. And when it comes to entertainment, it means making an effort to look for good and helpful websites, movies, songs, and shows.

> Finally, brothers and sisters, whatever is true, whatever is noble, whatever is right, whatever is pure, whatever is lovely, whatever is admirable—if anything is excellent or praiseworthy—think about such things.
>
> **PHILIPPIANS 4:8**

Paul tells us in Philippians 4:8 to think about things that are true, noble, right, pure, lovely, admirable, excellent, and praiseworthy. He tells us in 2 Corinthians 10:5 that we are to "take captive every thought to make it obedient to Christ." Our thoughts matter, and we need to be intentional about how we direct them.

According to Common Sense Media, American teenagers average nine hours of entertainment media use every day, not counting time spent at school or for homework. Tweens (8- to 12-year-olds) use an average of about six hours' worth of entertainment media daily.[12]

That's a lot of time. Is that time helping you become a true man? Or is it sabotaging your training?

MUSIC AND MEDIA

There are more and more ways to engage with media every day, from apps to video games to graphic novels. But for now, let's zoom in on music as our example of how to find and enjoy what will help you follow God.

Music is a wonderful form of art created by God. A whole book of the Bible is devoted to songs, and we learn in Revelation that there will be music in heaven for eternity. Music has an incredible ability to shape our emotions—to make us excited, to help us worship, to bring people together, even to lull babies to sleep. Many artists use their music to empower people or talk about social and religious issues that need to be addressed.

But that ability to shape our emotions is not always helpful. In the last decade, we have seen music lyrics become more violent and sexually explicit. Experts argue that this can cause problems in children and adolescents. Aggressive or violent music can push you to treat people more roughly. Music that talks about women as sexual objects can push you to treat them like that. Music that's all about getting drunk can push you to try alcohol yourself.[13]

Studies show that the average teenager listens to approximately forty hours of music in a given week.[14] This should make us think carefully when we are making our music selections. Even if your friends like listening to something, it still might not be helpful for you. In 1 Corinthians 10:23-24, Paul tells Christians, "'I have the right to do anything,'—but not everything is beneficial. 'I have the right to do anything'—but not everything is constructive. No one should seek their own good, but the good of others."

In other words, we do have freedom in Jesus to make many of own choices, but we need to make those choices based on love for God and for other people. There are certain songs you should definitely avoid, but there are others that will be more open to your judgement.

When you are choosing what to listen to, ask yourself these questions:

1. **Does this song tempt me where I'm weak?** If you are in a fight with your dad, it's not going to help you if you listen to a lot of angry music. Or, if you know that you can be greedy sometimes, listening to somebody singing about how rich he is might tempt you to love money even more.
2. **Does this song tempt the people around me where they are weak?** If I play this song in the car with my brother, will this song make it harder for him to stop swearing?
3. **Does this song help me think about what is true, noble, right, pure, lovely, admirable, excellent, and praiseworthy?** (Philippians 4:8) In other words, will it make you more excited about what God loves?

At some point, you're probably going to hear lyrics that will make it harder to be a true man. The challenge will be to recognize dangerous songs and keep them out of your playlist. Just because a song has a good beat doesn't make it appropriate. Be on your guard, and listen carefully to the message the lyrics are giving you. Be willing to find new music if you have to.

And don't forget, this doesn't just apply to music! Use these questions as you think about what shows to watch, what games to play, what comics to read, and what websites to visit.

What has been your favorite song recently?

_____

What do you like about that song?

_____

_____

_____

What is that song most excited about or focused on?

_____

_____

_____

What does that song tell you will make you happy?

_____

_____

_____

QUESTIONS

SOCIAL MEDIA AND YOUR IDENTITY

Technology and social media are a normal part of everyday life. We get information faster than ever before. We can learn almost anything at the touch of a screen. In some ways, this makes our life easier, but it also can create a new set of challenges.

Getting new friends or followers online can be exciting—and addictive. When we get too wrapped up in what people think about us online, we work harder and harder to make people like us. Sometimes we even put up fake versions of ourselves.

But your identity doesn't have to be in what you post, how many followers you have, or how cool you look online. You don't need other people to love you and make you matter. God already loves you.

If you trust in Jesus, here's what the Bible says about who you are: "I have been crucified with Christ and I no longer live, but Christ lives in me. The life I now live in the body, I live by faith in the Son of God, who loved me and gave himself for me." (Galatians 2:20) Christ Jesus loved you and gave himself for you, and now he is living in you!

When you are posting online, what's your goal? To look cool? To sound funny? Because Jesus already loves you, you don't have to say crazy or unkind things so that other people like you. That can free you to work and talk and go online for a different goal: to glorify God.

There's one more thing you need to know about the internet: what you post sticks around. Your words and pictures will still be there in 10 or 20 or 30 years. As you begin to use social media, remember that you are creating a digital footprint. That means everything you post and everything you do is building your reputation. Before you say something, ask yourself if you want it to show up when somebody (like a cute girl or your future boss) looks you up.

Social media platforms aren't always bad—they can be used to strengthen friendships and connect with people. But don't just use them because everybody else is using them. Ask yourself a few questions about any social media you want to use:

- » Will this really deepen my friendship? Does it help me love other people more?
- » Does this help me achieve my goals, or does it distract me from them?
- » When I leave that app or page, do I feel more joyful and content than when I logged on? Or do I feel dissatisfied, jealous, or angry?
- » Does this help me love God more, or does it distract me or tempt me away from him?

If you think something is hurting you more than it's helping you, log off or close your account. Ask a friend or parent to help you remember that you're not using it for a while. Perhaps a few weeks or a few years down the road, you can check in again and decide if it will be helpful at that time

GAMING YOUR TIME AWAY

Gaming is not a bad thing. But sometimes we can get so excited about the fictional adventures in the games that we get lazy about pursuing real adventures outside of the game. Don't let gaming consume so much of your free time that it takes the place of reality and real relationships. It is a time issue.

Here's a good rule of thumb—for every minute of game time, take a minute of real time outside or in conversation with an actual person.

You also need to make sure there are times in your days that are "noise free"—time when you aren't taking in a bunch of fast-paced information by looking at a screen, listening to music, or having a conversation. This time allows your brain to rest and gives you a chance to process what you played or watched, as well as what's going on in your life.

Video games have the tendency to make you feel like the hero. We all like that feeling, but it's not reality. The true story of the world, the story that we are all living in, has Jesus as the hero. Anything that takes away our attention from him and elevates us needs to be questioned. Ask yourself some hard questions about what you expose yourself to. Are your influences helping you live in a make-believe world, or the real world where Jesus is King?

If you have any social media accounts, what are the last three things you posted? Why did you post those things?

_____

_____

_____

_____

What type of media (like shows, movies, video games, books, music, or websites) do you usually spend the most time on?

_____

_____

_____

_____

QUESTIONS

NOTES ON SCREENS, STORIES, AND SONGS

Summarize the most important things you've learned.

_____

_____

_____

_____

_____

_____

_____

_____

_____

_____

Memorize and explain the key verse: Philippians 4:8.

_____

_____

_____

CHAPTER 11

Loving Your Family

You don't choose your family. They are God's gift to you, as you are to them.

Bishop Desmond Tutu, Cleric & Activist

During the Bosnian War, Air Force pilot Captain Scott O'Grady was monitoring a no-fly zone when he was shot down in enemy territory. He hid facedown while local soldiers found and examined his parachute, even shooting their rifles at it to try to scare him out—missing him by only a few feet. Undetected, he survived by sleeping under camouflage netting during the day, moving at night, and eating grass, leaves, and bugs.

Capt. O'Grady avoided patrolling Serbs until he made contact with NATO forces six days later. Military leadership chose the 24th Marine Expeditionary Unit to conduct the rescue mission, since it had trained extensively and could deploy right away.

At 4:40 in the morning, the order came to start the rescue. Fifty-one marines packed into two helicopters and took off from an aircraft carrier to retrieve Capt. O'Grady. They were accompanied by two helicopter gunships and two gun jets, with support from another eleven aircraft. The U.S. military was going to get their man.

After pulling O'Grady aboard their helicopter and flying low to the ground, the unit dodged two missiles launched by soldiers on the ground. Forty-five minutes later, they landed safely back on the aircraft carrier.[15]

 O'Grady survived his six days in enemy territory by using every piece of training he received and persevering through hunger, thirst, and fear. But in the end, Captain O'Grady had to rely on the help of his fellow soldiers to get him back home.

The same is true for you and your relationship with your family. At some point, you will face a difficult situation in your life, something you can't handle without help. The first place you should turn is your family.

THE VALUE OF FAMILY

Why is family so important? Because God designed the family unit. He provides families to protect you, teach you, and help you prosper. No matter how much your parents or siblings might drive you crazy, no matter how deeply they might disappoint or pain you sometimes, you are better off because you are growing up in a family, even if it's a divorced family, a single-parent family, or a step-family.

If one thing in your life is given to you without any input from you, it is your family. You didn't choose your family, but you still belong to your family forever. They may be the greatest source of stress, tragedy, and conflict in your life. They can cause you to lose sleep, and sometimes it can feel like they might make you lose your sanity. But your family also can be one of the greatest sources of laughter, healing, support, and love you will ever experience.

We all know we're supposed to love our families. But what does that look like as a teenager? In this chapter, we want to show you some practical ways to interact better with your family. Knowing how to interact better with your family can be a huge help, especially during the teenage years when how you understand and relate to them is changing.

HONORING YOUR PARENTS

Most teenagers experience more conflicts with their parents than they did as children. There are a lot of things that can tempt you to disrespect or fight with parents as a teenager. One of the most common temptations is feeling like your parents are treating you like a child.

Part of growing up is becoming independent. To some extent, it's natural to resist when parents and other adults impose what feel like childlike rules when we are not children. It's normal to start to develop your own ideas and preferences—ideas and preferences that may be different from those of your mom and dad. This is a key step in establishing your own identity.

> "Honor your father and mother"—which is the first commandment with a promise—"so that it may go well with you and that you may enjoy long life on the earth."
>
> **EPHESIANS 6:2-3**

But the command to respect your parents doesn't expire when you turn 13. The command to obey your parents is given specifically to children (Col 3:20, Eph 6:1), so there will be a day when you are an adult and might not obey your parents. But the command to honor your parents is given to everyone (Dt 5:16). No matter how old you are, and no matter how much you disagree with them, God commands you to honor your father and mother.

You can't control what your parents will do, but you can control your own attitudes, words, and behaviors.

So what does it look like to honor your parents as a teenager? Here are a few examples:

» Listening carefully to them
» Speaking to them with respectful words and a respectful tone (no sarcasm, defiance, delays, or excuses)
» Obeying them immediately
» Keeping your tone and body language positive

Unless they tell you to do something contrary to God's Word or the law, obey your parents. Your obedience to them does not depend on your liking what they are telling you to do. It is based simply on the fact that they are your parents, and God tells you to honor them.

FAMILY PRINCIPLES TO LIVE BY:
— Respect to your family
— Give thanks for your family
— Know that every family, and every individual, is flawed

Even when it doesn't feel like it, your parents are wiser than you are. Sure, they are probably out of touch with teen culture and clueless about some things, just as you will be one day. And sure, they make their share of mistakes. That doesn't mean they aren't wise. They've seen and experienced a lot of things you haven't. They know what your blind spots are, and they know where certain paths lead and how things usually turn out. They've watched you grow from an infant until now. They know you better than anyone else. They love you fiercely and want what is best for you.

It is in setting rules and boundaries—even in disciplining you—that parents shows how much they love you. It is not by being your buddy, or trying to make you happy, or giving you everything you want. When they set rules and boundaries, look for the love behind those rules. One day, you'll be grateful for the boundaries and rules they set. You'll see how that structure helped you to succeed and how their discipline sharpened your character. As crazy as it sounds now, you will even be glad they said no and grounded you.

But your relationship with them is not a one-way street of your obedience. You also need to communicate openly and often with your parents. They want to help you, but they can't read your mind. The responsibility is on you to make sure your parents understand what is happening in your life. Tell them about the pressures you are feeling from them or your friends. Tell them if you need some space, or if you wish they came to more of your games and didn't seem too busy for you.

Many parents back away from asking their teenage sons about what is on their hearts, about their needs and struggles, and the important things in life. Or they ask at times or in ways that might feel uncomfortable to you. When that happens, the burden for good communication about both the big and little things in your life falls on you.

Communicating openly and often with your parents shows that you trust your parents, and it helps them trust you. And the trust between you and your parents will make a huge difference in your relationship with them during your teenage years.

THINGS NOT TO DO WHEN IT COMES TO FAMILY

Don't measure their love for you by the gifts they give—or don't give—you. Even if they could give you everything you wanted, it wouldn't satisfy you. It would leave you entitled and spoiled. That new bike or drone or movie won't make you happy—the only thing that really satisfies is Jesus.

TWO WAYS TO EARN YOUR PARENTS' TRUST:
1. **Always be honest with them.** You can never lose their love, but you can lose their trust by being dishonest.
2. **Show responsibility.** Responsibility shows that you are growing up and maturing and can handle bigger privileges and opportunities.

Don't think their love depends on your performance. Even though they may cheer loudly for you, praise and brag about your accomplishments, and push you (maybe too hard) to achieve, your successes and failures don't affect their love for you. If you feel like their love depends on your performance, take the initiative to tell them.

Don't try to divide and conquer, getting one parent to overrule a decision the other has made. You are trying to turn them against each other for your own goals, but God calls us to sacrifice what we want to love one another. And that's how he loved you. He didn't try to use you to get what he wanted—he gave his life for you. Ask God to help you love your parents more than you love yourself and your goals.

Don't write off your parents' needs and wants. Your mom and dad are more than simply your parents—they are individuals with their own personalities, passions, and dreams. They have ups and downs, failures and frustrations. They get tired and stressed at their jobs and at home. They have friends who sometimes hurt or disappoint them. Take the initiative to figure out creative ways to tell them—and to demonstrate to them—that you love them.

Don't retreat too far and too often from your family. God wired you for connection and intimacy. You need that time and closeness with your family. If you retreat too frequently to your headphones, hide in your bedroom, or spend all your free time playing video games, you'll miss out on the relationships and memories you will one day cherish.

CREATIVE WAYS TO SHOW YOUR LOVE AND RESPECT TO YOUR PARENTS:

- Write an occasional letter to tell them you love them or are proud of them.
- Make them dinner and clean up the kitchen for them.
- Clean out the garage.
- Give them a night out while you watch your younger sibling(s).

What is causing you the most stress with your parents? Are there things your parents don't seem to understand about you? Have you talked with them about it?

_____

_____

Do you have a regular time that you and your parents talk about your life and relationship?

_____

_____

Are you showing honor to your parents? What can you do this week to show them honor?

_____

_____

QUESTIONS

LOVING AND RESPECTING YOUR SIBLINGS

Of course, a family is more than just parents. Brothers and sisters can fill your house with noise and chaos and conflicts. But they can also be your best allies in life.

As children created in the image of God (just like you), your siblings reflect God's amazing glory, and that means you should treat them with respect. 1 Timothy 5:8 tells us we are to protect and nurture our family, including our younger siblings: "Anyone who does not provide for their relatives, and especially for their own household, has denied the faith and is worse than an unbeliever."

You are called to look after the needs of all your siblings. God calls you to love them like he's loved you, and that's a high calling—loving them when it's difficult, when they're annoying, when you're exhausted.

It's not always easy. Jealousy can get in the way—maybe your sister is making better grades than you are, or your brother always seems to get better presents. If you are struggling with jealousy, look first at how much God loves you. He does not care who is better at school or who always knows the right thing to say—he purposely made you as you are, and he loves you.

TEN WAYS TO BE A GREAT BIG BROTHER:

1. Be kind. Look at how much Jesus loves you—enough to come all the way down from heaven and die for you. Remember how kind and patient he is to you. And ask for his help to show that kindness to your little siblings, no matter how annoying they sometimes are.

2. Be a sibling, not a parent. Giving them commands probably won't work. If you really need them not to do something, ask a parent to speak with them about it. That lets you focus on being their friend.

3. Give them some space. Sure, they can be annoying. But guess what? You can be, too. Everyone needs room to breathe.

4. Spend just five minutes focusing on them. You can make a difference by simply spending a few minutes a day talking to them about something—anything from a dream you had last night, to what shirt you should wear today. Ask them questions. They'll be psyched to share their opinions, and you'll see that every conversation doesn't have to end in a fight.

5. Spend more than five minutes with them. Once you've gotten the five-minute thing down, set aside some real time to spend with them. Play a board game, or take them to a movie you'd never go see without them.

6. Let them tag along sometimes. Take them with you to get something to eat or to explore the woods by your house. They'll feel included and cool because they get to hang out with you.

7. Set an example. Your little siblings look up to you. They watch the words you use, the way you treat your parents, the way you spend your time. Ask God to help you set a good example for them.

8. Use your skills. Practice basketball or soccer with them. Teach your brother or sister how to throw, catch, or ride a bike.

9. Teach them. Homework can be hard, and usually your parents are left to help them with it late at night after a hard day's work. You know how to help them and make it fun, too.
10. No younger siblings? You can still be a great brother or sister to a kid in need of a mentor!

LOVING YOUR OLDER SIBLINGS

But what about older siblings? God can teach us many things through our relationships with older siblings. They are just a few steps ahead of you on the road to adulthood, so they can have great advice on how to handle the teen years.

Your older siblings also provide both good and bad examples of making decisions. Pay close attention to how they handle different situations and learn from them. Follow the good examples, and show them God's grace and forgiveness when they set bad examples.

Ask to spend time with your older siblings. Relationships take work, and the relationships in your family are no different. Older siblings are often very busy, so take the initiative to ask them for time to hang out and do something fun together.

God uses your family to strengthen your compassion, love, and forgiveness. If you lived in a family that didn't test you, you wouldn't be growing. You wouldn't have as many opportunities to develop the attitude of a True Friend; you wouldn't have as many chances to serve. He's growing you through your siblings and parents and the struggles you are facing. Ask God to help you love and respect them.

Ask God to give you the patience to endure the inevitable conflicts and chaos that all families have, and pray for your parents and siblings. You may be surprised at how praying changes your feelings for your family and how you relate to them.

DIVORCE

As a teenager, you will feel many different emotions about your family. And if your parents are divorced, separated, or remarried, your emotions may be a lot more complicated and intense. You are not responsible for your parents and anything relating to their marriage, but their choices and actions have a big impact on you. Unfortunately and unfairly, marriage difficulties and changes can leave children feeling confused, worried, depressed, and angry.

For most boys whose parents have separated or divorced, there are three key questions that cause them anxiety:

1. **Is it my fault?** They wonder if they did something to cause the breakdown of the marriage. Feelings of guilt can consume them.
2. **Is there anything I can do to get my parents back together?** They feel pressure to fix it and frustration and despair when they can't.
3. **What will life be like after the divorce?**

Expect to wrestle with those questions. But more importantly, know the answers: you did not do anything to cause the divorce. There is nothing you can do to get them back together. And your life will change in some ways (but you can adjust and still live a great life).

While you will experience pain and various emotions, there are a few things you can do that can help. First, ask to have an active role in making decisions about the arrangements of your schedule. Tell them what times you prefer and what makes sense for how you divide your time. Similarly, request family meetings or family counseling to discuss tensions and problems the split or blended family is having. Studies have found that children who can have an active say in these things have a more positive experience than children who do not.

Ask your parents questions. In most cases, children are not given full explanations or a chance to ask questions, and this can lead to confusion.

Look for someone you can talk to about these family hurts, questions, and tensions. That's often a friend or a grandparent. Seeing a professional counselor can help to give you perspective, encouragement, and ideas for how best to handle this. Don't be too cool to seek help.

FATHERS

As we conclude this chapter on families, we want to talk to you about one especially important relationship in your family: your relationship with your dad. Adolescent boys crave time with their fathers. Ideally, each of you has a dad who can give you the time and attention you want and need. Unfortunately, many dads are very busy or don't live with their sons or just don't talk with their sons. Sometimes dads aren't sure if their sons want to talk about delicate or awkward topics. If it's possible, ask your dad to spend special one-on-one time with you. Ask him if, one night a month, just the two of you can go out to dinner or do some activity together. Ask him if the two of you can take a trip together once a year.

Your dad isn't perfect—and there are probably some things about him that disappoint or annoy you or maybe even really pain you—but he's been where you are.

Spending enough quality time together will often help you develop a relationship in which you can talk with your dad about anything. It's an incredible blessing to have a wise man, especially your father, with whom you can share any question or struggle and from whom you can learn about being a man. Unfortunately, it is also an uncommon blessing—most fathers and sons don't talk often and freely about the most important things in life.

Ask your dad about his boyhood and his relationship with his father. Ask him about girls and women and the different topics in this book. Ask him to read and discuss this book with you. Ask him about God; ask him what it means to be a man.

WHAT IF YOUR DAD ISN'T AROUND?

Many of you reading this book might be in a different situation. Some of you might have lost your father. Others have a father who is still living but not present in your life.

While this is not the situation God originally designed for a boy growing into manhood, there is good news. You have a Heavenly Father who has been with you since the beginning of your life and will be with you as you grow into a man. God the Father loved you so much that he sent his son Jesus to die on the cross so that you could have an eternal relationship with him. He promises to never leave us or forsake us. Although that may not change the difficult circumstances of your family, it can give you hope. You have a Father who loves you and cares deeply for you.

If you are in this situation right now, reach out to someone in your family first. We hope there is a man in your family who would be willing to talk through the journey to manhood with you. If there is not a family member to talk with, maybe there is a coach or teacher who would be willing to be your mentor. The important thing is to have someone who has been on the journey to manhood and who can help you prepare for what is ahead.

Here are some things to look for in a mentor:

>> He is a believer in Christ and seek to live for him.
>> He is willing to invest his time in mentoring you.
>> He lives a life that you would want to model.
>> He is willing to cast and model a vision of godly manhood for you.
>> He is willing to hold you accountable.
>> He is a student of God's Word.
>> He has a desire to love and serve others well.

A father to the fatherless, a defender of widows,
is God in his holy dwelling.

PSALM 68:5

How are you treating your siblings? What's one thing you can do this week to love each of your siblings?

_____

_____

_____

If you are living in a divorced, single-parent, or blended family, are you talking to anyone about the unique struggles that you are facing? If not, who could you talk to?

_____

_____

_____

QUESTIONS

Summarize the most important things you've learned.

_____

_____

_____

_____

_____

_____

_____

_____

_____

_____

Memorize and explain the key verse: Ephesians 6:2-3.

_____

_____

_____

NOTES ON LOVING YOUR FAMILY

CHAPTER 12

Why School Matters

It is not that I'm so smart. But I stay with the questions much longer.

Albert Einstein, Physicist

The mind is not a vessel to be filled, but a fire to be kindled.

Plutarch, Philosopher and Author

You know how if you're riding in a car that speeds up suddenly, you slam back into your seat? Now imagine accelerating to the speed of sound. When you are flying a plane that fast, the force can push the blood from your brain and make you pass out.

To fly fighter jets and other incredibly fast planes, pilots have to withstand certain levels of G-force, so they don't pass out while flying. G-force is the force of acceleration that pushes back on you like a weight, like when you slam back in your seat. 1 G is the speed of gravity, so it's how fast you would go if you were free falling.

But you don't want to wait until your plane is in the air to find out if your pilot is going to faint. That's where the centrifuge comes in. A centrifuge tests how much G-force a pilot can withstand before he goes into G-LOC (G-induced loss of consciousness). But the centrifuge doesn't just check what G-forces pilots can handle—it also lets them practice dealing with the G-forces before they are up in the air. Pilots are strapped into a little compartment on the end of a long arm, which spins around and around like a yo-yo on a string. It's a brutal test, and many would-be fighter pilots don't pass it.

To qualify to fly the fastest jets, pilots must learn from their training and their mistakes. The centrifuge is a challenge that forces pilots to push through a tough challenge and focus on the task at hand. Your upcoming years of school will be similar. You will need to endure some difficult challenges to move forward in becoming a man. Your school years will require you to pay attention, persevere, and learn as much as possible.

THE IMPORTANCE OF ATTITUDE

Let's face it: school can be stressful. Sometimes it's boring. Maybe you prefer weekends and summer to the structure of school. But since you have to be in school, and since you spend most of your waking hours at school, how can you make the most of school—and enjoy the time you spend there?

Here's a truth about a lot of things in life: your attitude often determines your experience. In other words, if you can develop a positive attitude toward school, you will enjoy it more. Controlling your attitude is an essential skill. People say that attitude determines altitude—in other words, how you think about things determines how high you go or how low you stay.

In this chapter, we'll give you a perspective on school that might change your attitude toward it, and then we'll give you some practical tips.

YOUR MIND NEEDS TRAINING

God created everything about you, including your mind. And he wants you to use it. Mark 12:30 says that he wants you to love him with all of your mind: "Love the Lord your God with all your heart and with all your soul and with all your mind and with all your strength."

We have found that the more we learn about the world—the smarter we get—the more it leads us to God. He designed you to think, reason, and understand. He designed you to explore, and he created a world and a universe worthy to be discovered. The grandeur, size, diversity, and complexity of the universe are powerful invitations to use our minds.

> I think, at a child's birth, if a mother could ask a fairy godmother to endow it with the most useful gift, that gift should be curiosity.
>
> **ELEANOR ROOSEVELT,** FIRST LADY

To use your mind well takes training. It doesn't happen automatically. Major league baseball players spend thousands of hours in the batting cage. They study pitchers. They lift weights. They field ground balls, learn to throw a curveball, and practice where to hit the ball in different situations. They listen to their coaches. They play pressure-filled games. They don't just show up one day at Yankee Stadium because they wanted to play major league baseball.

It's the same way with your mind. It needs training. You need to exercise it so that it doesn't become flabby, soft, and underdeveloped. You need people who can teach you. You need a place where you can exercise your mind. You need a mental batting cage or workout room. That place is called school.

Ideally, school would always be intellectually stimulating, a place for you to develop a thirst to learn about the world and its history. Science and math would excite you. Art and music would stir something in your soul. Your school experience would deepen the way you understand yourself.

WHAT ABOUT WHEN SCHOOL SEEMS BORING?

But sometimes, school is boring. It can feel like what you are learning has no connection to your life. You may wonder, "After all, how can Greek philosophers and gerunds and geometric theorems help me in life?"

What do you do when school seems boring and pointless? How you answer this question reveals a lot about your character, and it shows where you have opportunities for growth. Do you tend to mock or joke around (Prov 15:21)? Tune out (Prov 19:20)? Stop trying (Prov 18:9)?

Even when it's not your favorite subject, put your best effort into doing a good job. Do what you are assigned to the best of your ability. Why? Because this is your training ground for the challenges you'll face later in life. There will be many times as a man that you will have to engage in conversations and projects that you aren't excited about. People will look to you and rely on you to face those challenges with wisdom, respect, and integrity.

There are some things you can do to make school more interesting for you. Approach it with the mindset that you will make it an adventure. Remember, real men are adventurers. But sometimes the difference between drudgery and adventure is in how you look at it.

How you look at your life, school, and work matters. Your purpose should drive you. If our purpose in life is to glorify God in all we say and all we do, then every task matters. How we view our work each day matters as well.

There's a great old story about three workers who were assigned the same job but who looked at it very differently. The first worker was chipping chunks of stone away from large blocks. When asked what he was doing he responded negatively. He said, "I am hammering this stupid rock, and I can't wait to go home."

The second worker was working harder than the first and seemed focused on the task at hand. When asked about his job, he responded quickly: "I am molding this block of rock to help build a wall. It's tough work, and I will be glad when I am finished."

The final worker was different from the first two. He would pause after hammering away at the rock and admire the work he had completed. He worked and didn't break until he was satisfied with what he had accomplished. When asked what he was doing, he enthusiastically responded, "I am building a cathedral."

It's all about attitude. They were three different men doing the same job but with completely different attitudes.

What does it look like to have a positive attitude? Start by pushing yourself to think about how what you are learning connects to your life, to the world, or to what you've already studied. In your classes, ask your teachers tough questions. School is for your learning—not simply for your listening. As long as you are respectful, it's okay to disagree with what a teacher or the textbook says. The mark of a mature student is the ability to think for yourself, not just memorize what someone else says. Study other people's arguments to figure out when to believe them. Learn how to form your own opinions and beliefs and how to persuade people of them. When you decipher the arguments in your textbooks and essays, school becomes more exciting and relevant to your life.

Try to figure out how different subjects might fit together. Can you take an idea from a novel you are reading in English and apply it to something in history? How are musical scales like math? What is the relationship between science and faith? Thinking about questions like that can make classes more interesting and even adventurous.

So can seeking out people with different backgrounds and interests from your own. Make sure you listen humbly to people who have different experiences than you do—like people from another culture or just people who have lived a different life from you. And learn about religions and faith traditions different from your own. You'll learn that we all see and experience the world, including school, differently.

If you do these things, school will be more exciting for you. You may even find parts of it enjoyable. Now, however, some parts of it may still be slow at times. But God builds our character in mundane tasks. Doing your best in unexciting things builds self-discipline. It teaches you not to quit or take short-cuts. It makes you a hard worker. You develop a reputation as someone who is faithful and dependable.

If you develop those skills and characteristics, people will notice, and they will give you more responsibilities and opportunities for leadership. Those skills will come in handy one day in ways that you might not be able to imagine right now, enabling you to help others and execute a heroic purpose for your life. You'll probably look back at that boring time and realize that you were learning valuable lessons.

COACH BILLY DONOVAN'S ATTITUDE PLAN:

Always making today my best day

Taking pride in a job well done

Treating others with respect

Isolating my negative thoughts

Treating tasks as opportunities

Utilizing my talents every day

Doing the job right the first time

Expecting positive outcomes daily

Speaking well of others every day[17]

How hard you work in school will have a great impact on your future schooling and career. Students who make good grades, are involved in activities like sports or school government, and are good citizens are much more likely to get into their top choices for colleges. Colleges and graduate schools want to see whether you studied diligently, whether you persisted when work was hard, whether you were curious about different subjects. They will want to know how you spent your time—were you a leader in your school? Were you serving others? Were you teaming up with other students on a football game, a concert, or a school newspaper? And they will want to know what sort of a citizen you were.

When you finish school and start looking for your first jobs, you will be asked once again about how—and what—you did at school. And once again, those who were faithful and responsible at school will have a huge advantage.

> Many athletes have tremendous God-given gifts, but they don't focus on the development of those gifts. Who are these individuals? You've never heard of them—and you never will. It's true in sports, and it's true everywhere in life. Hard work is the difference. Very hard work.
>
> **JOHN WOODEN,** HALL OF FAME BASKETBALL COACH

Your choices today shape your future. But they can also impact other people. When you know how much God loves you, that can motivate you to work hard at school today so you have more opportunities to serve others as an adult. Working hard at school will give you the skills and knowledge to help the people and communities around you. Your math homework today isn't just homework—it's training you to calculate doses of medicine, architect a building, or figure out the missing pieces at a crime scene.

When you are motivated to do your work out of love for others and love for God, your work can show other people how amazing God is. In 1 Corinthians 10:31 Paul tells us, "So, whether you eat or drink, or whatever you do, do everything for the glory of God."

Is there a part of school that feels boring to you? What can that subject show you about God or his creation? Can you think of ways that subject connects to things you find interesting or exciting?

_____

_____

What are the right and wrong reasons to work hard in school? Do you think you are working hard? What's motivating you?

_____

_____

QUESTIONS

YOUR ACHIEVEMENTS DON'T DEFINE YOU

How you do in school can shape the options you have later, but it doesn't define who you are. You are not your grades or your activities. We tend to think that what we achieve shows who we are. It's one of the myths of manhood. But that's not your identity. You are not a math grade or an honor roll student. You are not a lacrosse champion or musician. You may achieve those things, or those things may be a part of your life, but that is not who you are.

You are God's child. You are precious to him based on what he did—not based on what you did or will do.

Do you know the story of Paul in the New Testament? Paul had just about every achievement you could brag about as a young Israelite man. He studied with the best teachers and got the best grades. And he even says that he was "blameless" in his obedience to the law. But those things weren't who Paul was. In fact, if his brilliant grades and perfect behavior made him proud or distracted him from Jesus, he counted them as worthless and annoying as garbage:

> What is more, I consider everything a loss because of the surpassing worth of knowing Christ Jesus my Lord, for whose sake I have lost all things. I consider them garbage, that I may gain Christ and be found in him, not having a righteousness of my own that comes from the law, but that which is through faith in Christ—the righteousness that comes from God on the basis of faith. (Philippians 3:8-9)

Pay attention to that last part. Your worth before God doesn't come from you, no matter whether you struggle with homework or ace every test. Your worth comes from Jesus, who loves you and gave his life for you.

If you are brilliant or athletic or artistic, that's a gift from God, and he can use that gift. But did you know he can use your weakness too? He didn't only pay attention when he was giving you things you are good at. He knows what's hard for you, and he can use those struggles. Listen to how Paul explains this:

> But God chose the foolish things of the world to shame the wise; God chose the weak things of the world to shame the strong. God chose the lowly things of this world and the despised things—and the things that are not—to nullify the things that are, so that no one may boast before him. It is because of him that you are in Christ Jesus, who has become for us wisdom from God—that is, our righteousness, holiness and redemption. Therefore, as it is written: "Let the one who boasts boast in the Lord." (1 Corinthians 1:27-31)

That doesn't mean you shouldn't work hard in school. God calls us to live for his glory in all that we say and all that we do, including your grades. Not everyone is a straight-A student, but everyone can give his best effort. But we can't make a good thing (like grades) the most important thing in our lives. Don't let who you are be defined by what you do. Your life should be defined by what God has done for you. He has paid the ultimate price for you because he loves you more than you can imagine.

WHAT HAPPENS WHEN YOU ARE LIVING FOR ACHIEVEMENTS AND ACCOMPLISHMENTS?

- You will feel anxious and depressed if you fail.
- You can be tempted to arrogance if you succeed.
- You will eventually learn that successes don't give your life meaning, and you will be confused and despairing.

If you know that your identity is defined by how God sees you, you also don't need to compare yourself to your classmates. God created you differently than he did your classmate who sits next to you in history class. There are so many ways to be smart—some people are brilliant at math, other people have an incredible ear for music, and still other people know just what to say to cheer somebody up. Some are more stereotypical ways to be smart, but all of those strengths are gifts from God, and they can all make a difference in the world.

We men are usually wired to be competitive and make comparisons. It can be an appropriate thing to compete, but don't let the results of your competition define how you think about yourself. Make the best grades you can, whatever they are. If you can let go of comparisons, your school years will be better ones.

It hurt me a great deal. It put a lot of pressure on me because I was at a young age and the writers around here and throughout the league started comparing me to [Ty] Cobb.

AL KALINE, HALL OF FAME OUTFIELDER

DO NOT OVER-SCHEDULE YOURSELF

Now we're moving to the everyday tips for how to succeed in school. First, don't over-schedule yourself. Too many teenagers get involved in too many activities. They end up tired and stressed and not doing anything as well as they should. Schoolwork suffers, and so do self-esteem, relationships, and health. As a general rule, limit yourself to one significant extracurricular activity at a time, and commit your best efforts to it. If you swim competitively, don't act in a play at the same time. Learn to say no to things that will overcommit you or compromise your well-being.

POSSIBLE EFFECTS OF DOING TOO MUCH:

- You will be too tired for homework or chores.

- You will miss out on opportunities for unstructured free play, which all boys need.

- You will miss opportunities for family fun.

- You will miss out on chances to serve others in the community.

RECHARGE AND REFUEL

Pay attention to eating healthy foods and getting enough sleep (at least nine hours a night). Even when you are sleeping, your brain is at work. It is sorting and storing information, replacing chemicals and solving problems. When you don't sleep enough, your brain doesn't adequately do those things, making it difficult to concentrate, read, and solve problems. You can't remember things as well, perform as well, or run as fast. Your immune system doesn't work as well, so you will get sick more often. You are more likely to be grumpy and irritable. You are more likely to get in arguments. In short, you sabotage yourself as a student and as a friend to others.

DEVELOPING GOOD STUDY HABITS:

— Make a plan for when and how you will accomplish your work.

— Make sure you have a quiet place without distractions. For most teenagers, the phone, TV, and computer are a distraction. You may be amazed at how much you can get done without distractions.

— Let your friends and family know about your homework schedule, and ask them to respect your time and not distracting you.

SCHOOL AND BECOMING A MAN

Of course, school is about more than studying. It is a training ground for your approaching manhood. It is a place of tests—not just academic tests, but tests of virtue and character. Are you up to the challenge?

Are you committed to telling the truth no matter what happens? Sometimes we feel like we are doing everything we can to win, even bending the rules. But that's not the example that Ruben Gonzalez set. In 1985, Ruben was considered to be one of the great new racquetball players in the world. His first pro tournament proved that. He was winning match after match, and that led him to the championship match in his very first tournament.

What happened in that final match stunned everyone. Ruben closed out the match and won the championship with a fantastic shot. It was so good that no one noticed that the ball hit the ground before it hit the wall, which is against the rules. The referee in the match even called the shot good.

The only person on the court who knew where the ball landed first was Ruben. He had a decision to make. He could walk off knowing the truth but still claiming the title, or he could tell the truth to his opponent and lose the title. Ruben decided to tell the truth and lost the title. When asked about it after the match, Ruben said, "It was the only thing I could do to maintain my integrity."[18]

One last thing: there will be hard times in school for you and everyone else, and it's okay to ask for help. There will be pressure and uncertainty and fear. Sometimes there will be failures and setbacks. Know that your teachers and administrators care about you.

Seek out a teacher or counselor you can confide in. Don't be too cool or tough to get the help you need. We adults know that school can be tough. Learn to lean on adults and on your family. More importantly, learn to lean on God.

QUESTIONS

Are you stressed at school? If so, what do you think is making you stressed? (Don't just think about outside reasons like pressure or assignments—look for inside reasons like your priorities and attitudes.)

_____

_____

What are you doing to serve your school to make it a better place? What can you do to demonstrate servant leadership this month at your school?

_____

_____

What do you think motivates you to do your schoolwork? In other words, how would you finish this sentence?

"If I didn't _____, I wouldn't go to school."

Summarize the most important things you've learned.

_____

_____

_____

_____

_____

_____

_____

_____

_____

Memorize and explain the key verse: Proverbs 18:9.

_____

_____

_____

NOTES ON WHY SCHOOL MATTERS

CHAPTER 13

Targeting True Success

Success is a lousy teacher. It seduces smart people into thinking they can't lose.

Bill Gates, Microsoft Founder

Money never made a man happy yet, nor will it. There is nothing in its nature to produce happiness. The more a man has, the more he wants.

Benjamin Franklin, A Founding Father of the United States of America

For college football fans, the first Wednesday of February is an important day: National Signing Day. This is when college football players announce which university they are committing to play for the following year. It is a day for families and friends to celebrate, but it is also a day when fans watch to see which players their favorite team gets for the upcoming season.

Around the country, hundreds of high school boys sit at a table that morning and put on the hat of the teams they choose to play for next season. To add to the suspense, some players even act like they are putting on one hat and then throw it to the side to put on the hat of their actual choice.

But did you realize that we are signing on to a team every day? We wake up each morning with a decision to make: who are we going to live for that day? Because of Jesus' finished work on the cross and his resurrection from the dead, we get the chance to live for his glory.

Which hat will you wear today? The world will give you plenty of chances to put your trust in other things like sports, grades, musical ability, girls, or popularity. God calls you in Joshua 24 to choose this day whom you will serve.

BEYOND HAPPINESS

Being happy is great. You're happy when school is canceled for a snow day, when you pitch a shutout in your baseball game, when you hear that a cute girl likes you, when summer finally arrives, when your friends are really nice to you, when your dad spends a lot of time with you, when people think you're cool, when your favorite football team wins, when you go to the beach, when the sky is blue, and when there's no homework.

The problem with happiness, as good as it is, is that it is often based on circumstances beyond your control. You can't make it sunny. You can't control whether your pro football team wins or whether that girl likes you. Happiness depends on things you cannot control. If your ultimate hope is in these things, they eventually will let you down.

Why, then, do we pursue happiness so intently? Ever since humans first sinned in the Garden of Eden, we have been cut off from God. In the core of our deepest being, we are sinful and broken, and we live in a fallen, messed-up world. That doesn't feel good. In fact, it hurts—we feel lonely, empty, afraid, and unsatisfied. So we naturally seek things that will make us feel happy, but it is sort of like taking a cough drop to cure cancer. It might make you feel better for a while, but it doesn't get rid of the disease.

So our main purpose or goal in life is not merely to be happy. We'll talk about the right goal in a minute, but first, we'll look at another misleading goal.

I've failed over and over and over again in my life,
and that is why I succeed.

MICHAEL JORDAN, NBA HALL OF FAME GUARD

What makes you really happy? Is it something you can control and count on?

_____

_____

_____

What do you think the difference is between happiness and joy? If you could just have
one, which one would you want and why?

_____

_____

_____

QUESTIONS

BEYOND SUCCESS

If happiness is the wrong purpose in life, then what about working to be successful? After all, can't we control how hard we work, and if we work hard enough and do the right things, shouldn't we be successful?

We like success. Winning is more fun than losing. We prefer to get A's rather than C's, to make the game-winning shot rather than miss it. It feels good to be recognized for winning a chess tournament or having your artwork chosen to be displayed at school. We aspire to be leaders, to make the honor roll, to win, to go to the best schools, and to get the best jobs.

Coaches play a crucial role in the success of an athlete. They have a chance to help a good player become amazing, or they can hurt a promising athlete. Many people consider John Wooden to be one of the greatest coaches of all time. In the world's view of success, he is at the top of the list. He won ten national championships in college basketball and coached some of the greatest players ever to play the game.

But Coach Wooden's version of success is different than the world's view of success. He rarely mentioned wins and losses when coaching. His focus was on preparing his players to be the best they could possibly be.

The problem with success, like happiness, is that we can make it the purpose of our lives when in fact it is not. Like happiness, success can let you down because you can't be the best all the time. Sometimes you'll miss shots, and sometimes others will beat you.

And even when you do succeed, it's not enough to satisfy you. And that's because God didn't create you to win. He created you to love him. And we can love him when we win, but we can also love him when he lose.

Although success (like happiness) is a dead-end purpose by itself, many teenage boys and men are addicted to it. Many of them get a taste of success, and they need more and more and more. They can start to define themselves by their successes or failures. For teenage boys, that means their identity can get wrapped up in things like what grades they get, how many games they win, how athletic they are, who they are dating, or how many friends they have. For men, this can turn into defining themselves by what their title is at work, how much money is in their bank account, or what they own.

When we start believing that who we are depends on what we accomplish, we feel intense pressure to perform for others, ourselves, and even God. And we end up putting our trust in ourselves rather than in him.

But you don't need to succeed to win God's approval. God doesn't love you for how hard you work or how many things you do right. Romans 5:8 tells us, "But God demonstrates his own love for us in this: While we were still sinners, Christ died for us." He didn't wait until you got an A or scored the winning goal. He loved you when you were still a helpless mess. (And even if we look successful, we're still quite messy a lot of the time—and he still loves us!)

How does the world define success?

_____

_____

How does God define success?

_____

_____

How are those two definitions similar? How are they different?

_____

_____

QUESTIONS

BEYOND MONEY

There's one more false goal we need to talk about: money and possessions. Sometimes we think that we'd be satisfied if we just had more stuff—a new video game, a better pair of cleats, a sports car.

This is called materialism. Materialism is not just having too many possessions. It starts when we link who we are with what we have. It is a heart issue. According to author Dave Harvey, "Materialism is fundamentally a focus on and a trust in what we can touch and possess."[19] In other words, we think our house (not God) keeps us safe, our toys (not God) make us happy, and our clothes (not God) make us valuable. We think money brings happiness, but it doesn't. Research has shown that, although as a country we are about twice as rich as we were fifty years ago, we are less happy than before.

If we think we need money to be safe and happy and valuable, we will be willing to do anything for it. We work for it. We put so much time and attention into earning more money and keeping it. It becomes our boss. But here's what Jesus says about that: "No one can serve two masters. Either you will hate the one and love the other, or you will be devoted to the one and despise the other. You cannot serve both God and money." (Luke 16:13).

Of course, money itself isn't evil—it is just a tool. If we use money well, it can be a good thing. You can use money to care for your family, to bless other people, and to make wise plans about the future. But make sure you make money your servant, not your master. Don't let it control you.

What are some examples of ways that money can help us love other people or serve God?

_____

_____

_____

173

QUESTIONS

What are the dangers and downsides of having a lot of money?

_____

_____

Do you get money from an allowance or a job? How can you use some of your allowance or money to help and serve others?

_____

_____

WHAT ARE YOU WORKING FOR?

When anything else becomes your master, it has become what the Bible calls an idol. If you studied ancient history, this might sound weird to you. Aren't idols those little statues people bowed down and sacrificed to? Yes, but "idol" also has a bigger meaning: a fake god. When we make something in our life more important than our relationship with God, it becomes an idol.

An idol is whatever you look at and say, in your heart of hearts, 'If I have that, then I'll feel my life has meaning, then I'll know I have value, then I'll feel significant and secure.'

TIM KELLER, AUTHOR AND PASTOR

An idol can be anything. Here are some examples:

- » Grades and success at school
- » Sports
- » Movies and entertainment
- » Family
- » Money
- » Physical beauty
- » Popularity
- » A romantic relationship
- » Political or social cause
- » Good behavior

Every day, we have an important choice to make. Will we worship the things of this world or the things of God? Our thoughts and minds should be totally consumed with bringing glory to God in all we say and do. Think about the first few words of our manhood definition: a real man glorifies God. That is your purpose in life. No matter where you are or what you have, your purpose remains the same: to live your life for the glory of God.

Your relationship with Jesus Christ must be the most important thing in your life. You need to know his love for you, and you need to love and follow him. This relationship is the only way to win the battle against the pressures of this world.

So now we've met three things competing for your heart: happiness, success, and money. Most boys and men know these idols very well. Many guys base their lives on these things. This mistake is probably the main reason that so many men today feel very confused and empty, have so many mid-life crises, and feel such a profound sense of doubt and despair.

Ever since they were boys, they've been told to climb the mountain of happiness, success, and money. They've worked hard and felt stressed for much of the climb, but they've learned the skills of the hiker and rock-climber and have performed all of the best moves with all of the best gear. But as they get to the top, up above the clouds, they realize that they've been climbing the wrong mountain. In the distance, they see a mountain that is far grander—a mountain they didn't know existed. As they wonder why no one told them they had set out for the wrong mountain, they feel a rumble beneath their feet, and their mountain starts to crumble.

GOD'S PURPOSE FOR US

God has a different mountain for you to climb. In fact, he'll do the hard part for you.

God tells us there is a different purpose for your life. It's simple but radical. Compared to what the world says, it's upside down and inside out.

For centuries, Christians have looked at the Bible and agreed that man's purpose is to glorify God and enjoy him forever. That means your purpose is to do things that bring him honor: things that tell him you know how powerful and good he is, things that demonstrate to others that you know and love him. In short, our purpose is to worship God each day in all parts of our lives—not just in church, but by how we act on Friday nights, how we think about and treat girls, and how we use our money and positions and opportunities.

YOUR ULTIMATE PURPOSE IS NOT ...
- To be happy or successful
- To be the best athlete
- To attend the most prestigious college
- To be comfortable
- To live in a huge house or drive an incredible car
- To have a pretty wife
- To have successful children

The second part of our purpose is to enjoy him. God is full of love. Out of his love, he has given us a beautiful world, and he has endowed us with many talents, gifts, and opportunities. Joy and happiness are very different. Happiness, as we saw earlier, depends on circumstances that are outside your control and that can change. Joy, on the other hand, is based on what God, who is unchanging, has done for you. It is based on knowing with both your head and your heart that God loves you and values you in a way that is much deeper and more profound than anyone on earth does. Your sins of yesterday, today, and tomorrow are forgotten and forgiven because Jesus took your punishment for you on the cross.

Realizing that your possessions and success will not give you significance frees you to develop a heroic purpose for your life—something big and grand and deeply rewarding. It frees you up to live as a Bold Adventurer—to seek opportunities and challenges that truly matter and make you feel alive. It frees you to pursue the work God has designed you for and called you to rather than just whatever earns the most money or praise.

GOD'S PURPOSE TAKES THE PRESSURE OFF

Living in God's purpose for your life does something else: it takes pressure off you. And pressure is something that most teenage boys and most men struggle with. It's hard to walk around thinking that who you are as a person depends on the grades you make, the games you win, the college you get into, and the promotions you get at work.

If you feel like you just can't measure up, if you feel like you are a mess on the inside, it's probably because you are. We don't deserve God's love. We sin and mess up all the time. But God loves us right in the middle of our unworthiness, and he already did the work to make a way for us to measure up to his love. If you trust in Jesus, the perfect life he lived is counted as your perfect life, and your mistakes are paid for by his death on the cross.

God tells us to find our value and worth in him. He assures us of his love. He tells us we were created in his image—not in the image of a straight-A student or CEO or rock star. We don't have to perform for God. We don't have to make certain grades from him to love us. We don't have to lead a company to get to heaven. We just have to trust in God and know that he loves us.

This righteousness is given through faith in Jesus Christ to all who believe. There is no difference between Jew and Gentile, for all have sinned and fall short of the glory of God, and all are justified freely by his grace through the redemption that came by Christ Jesus.

ROMANS 3:22-24

Let go of the need to perform and be perfect. Let go of the guilt when you fall short. Enjoy the fact that God loves you. When you know how much God loves you and how he will be with you even if you fail, you're free to work hard, hold high standards, and set big goals.

THE FEAR OF FAILURE

Of course, this is all easier said than done. Most people are consumed with the pursuit of happiness, success, and money. It usually begins in late childhood and really takes off in the teenage years. Most teenage boys develop an intense drive to perform and achieve—one that gathers more momentum in manhood. Teenage boys and men tend to have a great fear of failure. Often, that fear of failure motivates us even more than succeeding.

But failure isn't a dead end.

Look at the failures that many of the heroes of the Bible experienced. Adam and Eve had everything in the world and blew it. Abraham failed to trust God when he and his wife could not have children, and he lied to a king out of cowardice—twice! Moses got angry at God and never got into the Promised Land. Jonah defied God. Peter denied knowing Jesus.

You'll bomb a test, drop the big pass, and get rejection letters from colleges. You'll make big and little mistakes and commit a lot of sins. But your sins and mistakes are opportunities to experience the sweet grace and forgiveness of God. As weird as this sounds, thank God for times like these because you'll be a better person for them. It's healthy to fail and not get everything you want; it reminds us that God's purpose for our life is bigger and better—and sometimes different—than our own goals.

HOPE IN HARD TIMES

Some failures have bigger consequences—maybe you'll lose a job, damage a relationship, or get injured through reckless decisions. Other times, horrible things happen, and it's not your fault at all.

When your life gets hard, you can go in one of three directions. You can try to rely on your own strength, you can surrender to bitterness, or you can go to Jesus and ask him for help and comfort. You will find that when you turn to Jesus, no matter how hard your circumstances are, his grace, love, peace, and strength will see you through—even if it doesn't feel like it at the moment.

Tough times build our faith, reveal our hearts, and forge our character. In the upcoming years, each of you will experience pain and hardship. Your friends will disappoint and hurt you and sometimes desert you. A girl will break your heart. A loved one will die. You'll embarrass yourself, and doubt yourself.

The apostle Paul had a great perspective on happiness, success, and money. He was a powerful, wealthy, and respected man who had the finest education and the best things. By his world's standards, he was successful, but God interrupted Paul's life and showed him a much bigger purpose. Paul believed in Jesus and became a missionary. Eventually, he was arrested for sharing the gospel and thrown in prison, and it was there that he wrote this to his friends:

...for I have learned to be content whatever the circumstances. I know what it is to be in need, and I know what it is to have plenty. I have learned the secret of being content in any and every situation, whether well fed or hungry, whether living in plenty or in want. I can do all this through him who gives me strength.

PHILIPPIANS 4:11B-13

We hope you set out to climb the right mountain. The path is not performance or success, but humility and surrender. Set aside your ego—and the myth that men have to be strong and successful on their own—and admit to God you can't do it yourself. Give your heart to Christ. Ask God to give you the new heart he promises (Ez 36:26). It will change your teenage years and your life as a man.

What are your idols? What are the things in your life that it would be very difficult to be without?

_____

_____

Think about some ways you failed in the past year or few years. What did God teach you?

_____

_____

What do you think you are living for right now? Don't just give the right answer—look at how you spend your time, energy, and money.

_____

_____

What steps can you take to help your goals line up with God's goals?

_____

_____

QUESTIONS

Summarize the most important things you've learned.

_____

_____

_____

_____

_____

_____

_____

_____

_____

Memorize and explain the key verse: Philippians 4:11b-13.

_____

_____

_____

NOTES ON TARGETING TRUE SUCCESS

CHAPTER 14

Cleared for Takeoff

"I firmly believe that any man's finest hour, the greatest fulfillment of all that he holds dear, is that moment when he has worked his heart out in a good cause and lies exhausted on the field of battle—victorious."

Vince Lombardi, Hall of Fame Coach

Chuck Yeager might be the most famous pilot of all time. He is best known as the pilot who broke the sound barrier, flying faster than the speed of sound. But before then, he logged thousands of hours in hundreds of planes. Yeager was known for his hard work, grit, and determination.

He learned anything and everything he could about planes and flying. He wanted to make sure that he knew everything that could go wrong and how he could fix it. This allowed him to stay calm under pressure. Yeager's passion and hard work allowed him to be one of the most successful pilots in U.S. history.

We hope that you take this book and read over it again and again like Chuck Yeager did with his plane manuals. Reading this book can give you a clearer sense of what it means to be a man—and it can warn you about some of the challenges you will face in the upcoming years. The teenage years are an exciting time of growing independence and exploration, new passions and possibilities. They are years when you are establishing your identity, beliefs, and values. It is a critical time in your life!

MANHOOD: A real man glorifies God by seeking an adventurous life of purpose and passion as he protects and serves others.

We pray that your life will be lived to the glory of God and marked by seven virtues:

- » The True Friend: Stands Up and Stands By
- » The Humble Hero: Uses Gifts for God's Glory
- » The Servant Leader: Takes Initiative for Others
- » The Pacesetter: Sets the Example
- » The Bold Adventurer: Goes Courageously
- » The Noble Knight: Lives Honorably
- » The Faithful Follower: Is Loved by God

God designed you to live a fulfilling and purposeful life as a teenager and a man. Fulfilling the purpose God has in mind for you depends not simply on following certain advice and rules, though that's part of it. The most important thing is developing a personal relationship with God. It is experiencing fellowship with him and the fullness of his love. It is having a heart for the Lord. God wants your heart more than merely your words or behavior.

> Give up yourself, and you will find your real self. Lose your life, and you will save it. Submit to death, death of your ambitions and favorite wishes every day and death of your whole body in the end: submit with every fiber of your being, and you will find eternal life ... Look for yourself, and you will find in the long run only hatred, loneliness, despair, rage, ruin, and decay. But look for Christ and you will find him, and with him everything else thrown in.
>
> **C.S. LEWIS,** AUTHOR

In this final chapter, we will issue two challenges. Along the way, we will ask you questions—answer them honestly. This is the only way you can truly see where you are on the path to authentic manhood. The flight plan has been issued. It is up to you to get in the seat and let God take control of your journey.

CHALLENGE #1: ARE YOU READY TO MAKE THE COMPLETE COMMITMENT?

You are committed to a lot of things right now. Some guys are committed to sports. Others are committed to art or music. While those are good things, being completely committed to becoming a godly man is far more important.

The journey to real, authentic manhood is not easy. It will require you to make decisions that might not be popular. It will force you to take a stand even when nobody else is willing. We are to surrender our lives to God and live our lives in service to him. Jesus is completely committed to you. He gave his life for you. Will you live for him?

Becoming a godly man requires complete commitment. Are you willing to make that commitment?

> You, my brothers and sisters, were called to be free. But do not use your freedom to indulge the flesh; rather, serve one another humbly in love.
>
> **GALATIANS 5:13**

CHALLENGE #2: WILL YOU BE SHAPED BY GOD'S WORD?

Commercials want you to buy certain products. Websites want you to use their services. Magazines draw your attention by placing good-looking women on the cover. The more time you spend watching, reading, or listening to something, the more it will shape your life.

The journey to manhood is no different. You cannot allow the world's view of manhood shape your thinking. According to the Barna Research Group, the average Christian spends about ten minutes per day with God. The average American spends four hours each day watching television or on the computer. What do you think is influencing you more?

The journey to godly manhood will require you to commit to spend significant time in God's Word. It will also require you to guard against outside influences that can twist your view of manhood. Spend time in God's Word and allow it to shape you. This will equip you to make decisions based on the Word of God and not the ways of the world.

This is a difficult challenge. Are you willing to spend less time on yourself so that you can pursue the adventure God has in store for you?

The journey to manhood will be no different. You will be tempted to take the road of success and popularity in place of respect and admiration. Take the road that God calls us to, the road to glorify and honor God in all we do. This road calls us to be Faithful Followers, stay the course, and give up control of our lives. Are you willing to hand over control of your life to God?

WE ARE NOT ON THIS JOURNEY ALONE

The challenge has been issued. Are you ready to accept it?

We were not designed to go on this journey alone. Living out the virtues of manhood, making the right choices about drinking, drugs, and girls; getting along with your family and friends, and following God—these are best done alongside others.

God has given us parents, friends, and mentors to help us navigate the journey. Gather your True Friends and make a commitment to each other. This will be extremely helpful as you begin this journey. The road is long, and it helps to have traveling companions.

But it's not just your friends, parents, and teachers who are with you on this journey. The good news of God's Word promises us we will find God if we truly seek him. He promises us his Holy Spirit to empower and direct and comfort us. He promises us new hearts and eternal salvation through his Son, Jesus Christ. He assures us that, in Christ, we are worthy and good—the question every man eventually wrestles with. He tells us what it means to be a man.

On your journey to manhood, you will fail sometimes. That's okay. God's love for you is not based on your successes, and you can't lose it by failing. God loved you before you did anything for him, and he died to pay for all of your failures. When you fall short of being the man God wants you to be, don't give into despair or just sit around feeling guilty. Ask for his forgiveness and help.

God doesn't want us to be driven and motivated by guilt and fear. He wants us to receive his love, sacrifice, and perfect record.

What about you? Are you letting God work in you? Do you understand his grace and the gift he is presenting you?

God is seeking you, and you have the opportunity—and the choice—to seek and find him. You can accept his gift of Jesus Christ. You can be motivated by gratitude or by guilt. You can exchange a life of achieving for receiving. You can trade in despair for joy.

By confessing your sins and professing Jesus Christ as your Lord and Savior, you can receive his perfect record. You can experience the joy and peace that comes with knowing that, no matter the circumstances, you are known and loved by God and will live with him forever. Knowing that frees you up to live differently—to share your love more freely, to be more adventurous, to live purposefully, to pursue passions, to serve and protect others, and to create a just and kind society. In short, knowing God's love frees you to be the man God designed you to be.

The mission is set before you. Buckle up—it is going to be a great flight!

Summarize the most important things you've learned.

_____

_____

_____

_____

_____

_____

_____

_____

_____

_____

Memorize and explain the key verse: 1 Samuel 2:30.

_____

_____

_____

NOTES ON CLEARED FOR TAKEOFF

NOTES

Chapter 2—The Six Myths

1. "The Mystery of Flight 19." NAS Fort Lauderdale Museum. August 3, 2010. Accessed June 12, 2018. https://www.nasflmuseum.com/flight-19.html.

2. Kimmel, Tim. *Raising Kids for True Greatness: Redefine Success for You and Your Child.* Nashville, TN: W Publishing Group, 2006.

Chapter 3—The Seven Virtues

3. Piper, John. "Glorifying God . . . Period." Desiring God. July 15, 2013. Accessed June 12, 2018. https://www.desiringgod.org/messages/glorifying-god-period.

Chapter 4—Finding Your True Friends

4. Risner, Robinson. *The Passing of the Night: My Seven Years as a Prisoner of the North Vietnamese.* Duncanville, USA: World Wide Printing, 1999.

Chapter 5—Resisting Peer Pressure

5. "Fighter Pilot Newest Canadian Astronaut." *Air Force Crew Brief 07* (Summer 2009): 15.

Chapter 6—The Dangers of Alcohol and Drugs

6. "Jet-winged Adventurer Ditches in Atlantic, Unhurt." ABC7 New York. November 25, 2009. Accessed June 12, 2018. http://abc7ny.com/archive/7139430/.

7. Office of Adolescent Health. "Adolescents and Tobacco: Trends." HHS.gov. September 23, 2016. Accessed June 13, 2018. https://www.hhs.gov/ash/oah/adolescent-development/substance-use/drugs/tobacco/trends/index.html.

8. National Institute on Drug Abuse. "Research on the Use and Misuse of Fentanyl and Other Synthetic Opioids." NIDA. June 30, 2017. Accessed June 13, 2018. https://www.drugabuse.gov/about-nida/legislative-activities/testimony-to-congress/2017/research-use-misuse-fentanyl-other-synthetic-opioids.

9. Frankel, Joseph. "The Hard-to-Trace Ingredient Behind Skyrocketing Cocaine Deaths." The Atlantic. May 03, 2018. Accessed June 13, 2018. https://www.theatlantic.com/health/archive/2018/05/americas-opioid-crisis-is-now-a-fentanyl-crisis/559445/.

Chapter 8—Understanding Puberty

10. Abridged from *Choosing the Best: A Values-Based Sex Education Curriculum.* Atlanta, GA, 1993.

Chapter 10—Screens, Stories, and Songs

11. Coram, Robert. "John Boyd - USAF, The Fighter Pilot Who Changed the Art of Air Warfare." Aviation History Online Museum. November 2002. Accessed June 13, 2018. http://www.aviation-history.com/airmen/boyd.htm.

12. "Landmark Report: U.S. Teens Use an Average of Nine Hours of Media Per Day, Tweens Use Six Hours | Common Sense Media." Common Sense Media: Ratings, Reviews, and Advice. November 03, 2015. Accessed June 13, 2018. https://www.commonsensemedia.org/about-us/news/press-releases/landmark-report-us-teens-use-an-average-of-nine-hours-of-media-per-day.

13.   "Impact of Music, Music Lyrics, and Music Videos on Children and Youth." PEDIATRICS 124 (November 1, 2009). Accessed June 13, 2018. doi:10.1542/peds.2009-2145.

14.   Ibid.

Chapter 11—Loving Your Family

15.   Claes, Bjorn. "One Amazing Kid - Capt. Scott O'Grady Escapes from Bosnia-Herzegovina." F-16.net. 2018. Accessed June 13, 2018. http://www.f-16.net/varia_article10.html.

Chapter 12—Why School Matters

16.   Swindoll, Charles R. *Strengthening Your Grip: Essentials in an Aimless World.* Toronto: Bantam Books, 1986.

17.   Peterman, Scott. "Billy Donovan's Daily Attitude Plan | Uncategorized." Mens Basketball Hoopscoop. June 10, 2010. Accessed June 13, 2018. https://www.mensbasketballhoopscoop.com/billy-donovans-daily-attitude-plan/.

18.   Garland, Nick. "Walk in Integrity." Nickgarland.me. January 31, 2017. Accessed June 13, 2018. http://nickgarland.me/2017/01/31/walk-in-integrity/.

Chapter 13—Targeting True Success

19.   "Getting to the Heart of Materialism." Crossway. December 22, 2009. Accessed June 13, 2018. https://www.crossway.org/articles/getting-to-the-heart-of-materialism/.

Made in the USA
Columbia, SC
27 June 2020